SECRETS OF PARIS

Power over Cancer (1996)
Crossdressing (1996)
How to Conquer Arthritis (1996)
High Blood Pressure (1996)
How To Stop Your Doctor Killing You (1996, revised edition 2003)
Fighting For Animals (1996)
Alice and Other Friends (1996)
Spiritpower (1997)
How To Publish Your Own Book (1999)
How To Relax and Overcome Stress (1999)
Animal Rights – Human Wrongs (1999)
Superbody (1999)
Complete Guide to Life (2000)
Strange But True (2000)
Daily Inspirations (2000)
Stomach Problems: Relief At Last (2001)
How To Overcome Guilt (2001)
How To Live Longer (2001)
Sex (2001)
We Love Cats (2002)
England Our England (2002)
Rogue Nation (2003)
People Push Bottles Up Peaceniks (2003)
The Cats' Own Annual (2003)
Confronting The Global Bully (2004)
Saving England (2004)
Why Everything Is Going To Get Worse Before It Gets Better (2004)
The Secret Lives of Cats (2004)
The Cat Basket (2005)
The Truth They Won't Tell You (And Don't Want You To Know) About The EU (2005)
Living in a Fascist Country (2006)
How To Protect and Preserve Your Freedom, Identity and Privacy (2006)
The Cataholic's Handbook (2006)
Animal Experiments: Simple Truths (2006)
Coleman's Laws (2006)
Secrets of Paris (2007)

novels
The Village Cricket Tour (1990)
The Bilbury Chronicles (1992)
Bilbury Grange (1993)
Mrs Caldicot's Cabbage War (1993)
Bilbury Revels (1994)
Deadline (1994)
The Man Who Inherited a Golf Course (1995)
Bilbury Pie (1995)
Bilbury Country (1996)
Second Innings (1999)
Around the Wicket (2000)
It's Never Too Late (2001)
Paris In My Springtime (2002)
Mrs Caldicot's Knickerbocker Glory (2003)
Too Many Clubs And Not Enough Balls (2005)
Tunnel (1980, 2005)
Mr Henry Mulligan (2007)

as Edward Vernon
Practice Makes Perfect (1977)
Practise What You Preach (1978)
Getting Into Practice (1979)
Aphrodisiacs – An Owner's Manual (1983)

with Alice
Alice's Diary (1989)
Alice's Adventures (1992)

with Donna Antoinette Coleman
How To Conquer Health Problems Between Ages 50 and 120 (2003)
Health Secrets Doctors Share With Their Families (2005)

Secrets of Paris

Paris for Beginners:
An Insider's Guide

Vernon Coleman

Chilton Designs

Published by Chilton Designs, Publishing House, Trinity Place,
Barnstaple, Devon EX32 9HG, England.

First published by Chilton Designs in 2007

ISBN: 978-1-898146-02-5

A catalogue record for this book is available from
the British Library.

Printed by Antony Rowe Limited, Wiltshire

Contents

Dedication

There's a good reason for this book being written in the first person plural rather than the first person singular. The reason is Donna Antoinette Coleman. She has worn out many pairs of shoes, and gained countless blisters, tramping the streets of Paris and helping me research this book. With Donna Antoinette by my side Paris always looks at its beautiful best.

Secrets of Paris is dedicated to her with my thanks as well as all my love. It is her book just as much as it is mine. (Though responsibility for errors or omissions is *all* mine.)

Preface

There are some places in Paris which every tourist visits. Sacre Coeur, the place du Tetre, the Louvre and the Champs-Elysées are on everyone's list of 'must-see' sights. You can't go to Paris without standing on a traffic island at the bottom of the Champs-Elysées and taking a photograph of the traffic racing up towards the Arc de Triomphe. It's what everyone does. You then have to walk up and down. Everybody does. No reason. They just do.

Nor can you visit Paris for the first time without joining the throngs queuing to go up the Eiffel Tower. (Well, you can. But it would be a pity. And, remember, if you end your trip to Paris with heaps of things left to do, then you will always have something to look forward to for your next visit.)

But, wonderful as these iconic places are (and they all are wonderful and well worth a visit) there are many other places in Paris which are a real delight to visit but which the official tours don't and won't take you to. Nor will the usual guidebooks recommend them.

We've spent years putting together this list of our favourite Parisian secrets, and we're confident that if you spend a little time following our suggestion to wander off the beaten track, and look at Paris from a slightly different angle occasionally, you won't regret it.

Most guidebooks are filled with dull and immediately forgettable information about the dates buildings were commissioned, and the dates their architects were born and died. You might, for example, discover that Paris used to be called Parisea and before that was known as Lutetia. But, quite frankly, who cares? Unashamedly and unapologetically *Secrets of Paris* is designed to give you the sort of gossipy, genuinely helpful information a friend who knows Paris would give you. Paris is one of the easiest cities in the world to understand and to find your way around – once you know the secrets. We've also included a section designed to introduce to you the French; to help you learn how to enjoy Paris and to understand the Parisians.

You'll see that this book contains none of the advertisements or overt recommendations which so often seem to be scattered in modern guidebooks. This means that as authors our only allegiance is to you, the reader. And we would also like to assure you that we have received no sponsorships nor freebies nor cut-price anythings (nor have we ever tried to obtain any). Where we recommend particular services or shops it is purely because we have found them to be worth recommending.

Finally, we've tried to make this a book you'll find fun to read as well as to use as a reference guide.

Enjoy Paris. It's difficult not to.

Vernon Coleman, Paris, November 2006

Part 1: The Planning

1. How to get to Paris

If you are travelling to Paris from the UK we don't think you should contemplate going there by plane unless you live more than two or three hours away from London. From most places in the UK, the easiest way to get to Paris is to travel first to London (or Ashford) and then go under the Channel by Eurostar. It really is the most convenient way to get there. (We still prefer to refer to the stretch of water separating Dover from Calais as the English Channel, though doubtless in deference to the requirements of the European Union, English civil servants at the Foreign Office now apparently refer to it as La Manche.)

Travelling by plane may be cheaper (if you manage to get one or two of those absurdly cheap tickets which are constantly being advertised) but these days there really isn't any point in going anywhere by plane unless the train journey is likely to last at least a day. The delays at airports are so common (and so interminable) that you'll get there quicker and more reliably if you travel by train. This is particularly true if you intend to travel from a large metropolitan airport. (Passengers using smaller airports, situated well away from the centre of Government and the itchy fingers of trigger-happy, publicity-hungry Ministers, are far less likely to be inconvenienced by finding the airport forecourt blocked by a congregation of tanks.) Although the security guards at British and

French railway stations have become considerably more officious in recent years they are still nowhere near as bad as the Gestapo guards employed to confiscate nail files and bottles of mothers' milk at European airports. We readily confess that we find it difficult to entrust ourselves to the custody of airline pilots who are so frail that they feel unable to protect themselves against 85-year-old passengers armed only with nail files.

The Eurostar train gets into the station Gare du Nord which is situated within a thirty minute taxi ride of anywhere in central Paris, unless the taxi driver gets lost or decides to take you to see the sights first which, you will discover, he probably will.

If you travel first class on Eurostar the staff will usually give you something to eat, a cup of coffee or tea and, best bit of all, a most welcome and soothing hot towel after you've eaten. They will also give you a glass or two of moderately drinkable alcohol. We find that with the aid of wine our ability to speak French is dramatically enhanced. Once in Paris, we climb into our taxi imbued with tremendous confidence in our ability to speak the local language in the way we always wanted to be able to speak it. Sadly, the Parisians we meet are rarely advantaged in the same way and they usually fail to understand a word we say. Perhaps they would do better if they too had enjoyed a glass or two of claret.

In contrast to the train, a flight to Paris will leave you stranded in a distinctly unpleasant, deserted and provincial wasteland from which you will find it difficult to escape. There is a special coach service from the airport into Paris (known as the Roissy bus) but the main centre-of-the-city stop is at the Opera and unless you are staying within walking distance of this point you will still have to find some other form of transport to take you to your hotel.

The Roissy bus is quite cheap and fairly efficient but it does get stuck in traffic and it often gets rather unpleasantly crowded. A coach which can provide adequate accommodation for thirty or so normal travellers becomes unbearably claustrophobic when it contains two or three Americans travelling with their luggage. Taxis from the airport to the city centre will eat up a good chunk of your cash and, unless you are lucky with the traffic, a good chunk of the time ear-marked for sitting in cafés, wandering through parks or window shopping on the rue St Honoré or the rue de Rivoli.

2. Don't go to Paris in August

However tempted you may be by the special offer prices available from your travel agent, don't, please don't, go to Paris in August. Almost any other month of the year will be fine but going to Paris in August is not a good idea.

Unless you have lived in Paris, or explored away from the main tourist haunts you will probably have no idea of the extent of the August shutdown. Even in the tourist areas many shops and attractions are closed. To the French, August is a month for holidays away from the city.

We, too, had no idea just how complete the shut down is until we discovered that we had a leak in our Parisian apartment. We have a 24 hour a day, 7 days a week service contract with a plumbing company and the idea is, of course, quite simple. If we have a plumbing problem we ring them and they send someone round to deal with it. For this service we give them money.

We should have known that something was wrong from the fact that we had to ring five times before anyone answered the telephone.

'We have water leaking from a pipe,' we told the rather bored sounding man who eventually picked up the receiver.

'What is your address?' he asked.

We told him.

'Someone will come in September,' he said.

'September!' we cried, aghast. 'We have water pouring from a leaky pipe.'

'It is August,' he explained. We could hear the shrug of indifference. 'Everyone is on holiday.'

What was so surprising was his astonishment that we should expect a plumber to be available in August.

In the end we decided, in the best French fashion, that the leaky pipe was not our problem. It was the problem of the people in the apartment below. And they, of course, were away for August.

15

You are unlikely to need a plumber if you're going to Paris on holiday. But August is still not a good time to visit. Not only are many cafés, bars and shops closed for the month but you will also find that the streets and parks are empty of Parisians and full of sweaty Americans. If you visit Paris in August you will come away with a very low view of the place.

The other reason for not going to Paris in August is the weather. August has always been a hot month in Paris but since global warming took a hold on the world the temperatures in the capital have become unbearable (July has now become too hot, too). A candle in our apartment actually drooped and melted into a shapeless lump of wax during one particularly nasty heat wave. Even the pigeons were feeling too knackered to fly. They just sat on ledges and did nothing. The heat is, of course, why the Parisians spend August somewhere else. And it's why you, too, should keep away. Ignore the fact that hotels offer good prices in August. The prices are low then for a very good reason. If you do not follow this advice you will regret it. 'We should have done what the book said,' one of you will say, as you both lie exhausted and soaked on your hotel beds. 'But it was 10% cheaper,' the other will reply. And then the row will start and you will end up paying a fortune to abandon your holiday and go back home.

3. Make sure you wear comfortable clothes and shoes

Wear comfortable shoes. And wear comfortable clothes – preferably with loads of zip pockets. But if you don't want the Parisians to depress you with their sneers we suggest that you wear something that is reasonably chic. Don't wear shorts or anything that would look well-suited to a Spanish beach. The Parisians are offended by anything made out of shiny nylon or material which contains pictures of palm trees. We don't wish to offend you by mentioning these things; our aim is simply to help you avoid finding yourself the object of scorn and pity.

If you can't stuff everything you need into your pockets, and you need to take a bag with you when you are out and about, make sure that it is light and has zip pockets. Zips on pockets and bags will provide you with some protection against pickpockets (especially if the zips stick a bit and are difficult to open) but we suggest that you carry valuables (passport and money) in a hidden money belt. Just keep enough money for each day's needs in the wallet you carry in your pocket or handbag. This, incidentally, will be the wallet you hand over if you are robbed – it is what we call a 'mugger's wallet'. To make your 'mugger's wallet' look authentic add a couple of old, expired membership cards, which will be no loss to you and of no value to anyone else. Our mugger's wallets contain: a membership card for a video library which was converted into a Chinese take away in 1996, an impressive-looking discount card for a fish and chip shop which has been a mobile phone shop since 1994 and an expired entrance pass for the Casino in Monte Carlo. (Paris is no worse than any other city for street crime, and it is much safer than most. But we prefer to take precautions.)

4. Be careful when choosing a hotel (it's position that counts)

Hotels in Paris are, on the whole, surprisingly cheap. (You can, of course, spend a fortune if the Government or your company is paying the bill, and you desperately need a third of an acre of lushly carpeted real estate.) It is the position of your hotel that is crucial. You must stay somewhere in central Paris. Ignore all those smart new hotels which promise you modern glass and steel, an Olympic swimming pool and easy access to the city centre via the French railway system. Stay in one of these and you will spend more time underground than you will spend admiring Paris. You need to be in central Paris.

The best arrondissements for you to stay in are the 1st, 2nd, 6th, 7th or 8th. Alternatively, lay out a map of Paris in front of you. Find three points: the place de l'Opera, the Jardin du Trocadero (just west of the Eiffel Tower) and Notre Dame. Now draw a vertical line through the Jardin du Trocadero, a horizontal line through the place de l'Opera and vertical and horizontal lines through Notre Dame. You will have created a box on your map. Unless you have a particular reason to stay elsewhere we suggest that you look for a hotel that is situated within the box. You'll find plenty of choice.

With your base in one of our recommended arrondissements, or within this rectangle, you should be able to walk anywhere you want to visit.

If you have booked your own hotel (rather than using a tour operator) it might be worth asking if there are any discounts. If there has been any sort of international incident in recent months the prices are likely to be down because of the absence of American tourists. The Americans are, by and large, extremely nervous people and they don't like to travel if they have just read about some sort of incident in a foreign place. Their knowledge of geography is sketchy at best and they think that everywhere which is not actually part of America is all in one place called 'Foreign'. This means that if a bomb has gone off in Istanbul they will all cancel their trips to Brazil, Australia and France and stay at home and cower in the nearest shopping mall. (The poor souls are far too stupid to realise that America is, with the possible exception of the many places which the Americans have invaded, the most dangerous place on earth.) The advantage of this to you is twofold. First, you will probably be able to persuade your hotel to offer you a room at a cut-price rate. Second the city of Paris won't be full of swaggering, overweight Americans taking up the pavement and spoiling the view with their polyester-wrapped behinds, and the parks won't be packed with overweight American joggers, obese explosions in fluorescent shellsuits, huffing and puffing and wheezing and threatening to expire at any moment as they struggle along at sub-walking pace.

5. Cash or travellers' cheques?

We never bother with travellers' cheques; considering them to be an expensive waste of time and money. And we don't use British credit cards in France except in emergencies. We take nice crisp euro notes.

Technically, it is rumoured that shops are only allowed to accept payment in cash for items which cost 100 euros or less. But, not to our surprise, we have not yet heard of anyone in France prepared to turn down a cash payment.

If you do decide to take cash we suggest that you carry your cash in several places upon your person. Don't leave money in your hotel or keep it all in your bag. Money belts are cheap to buy and effective to use. (Do not, however, put anything metal in them. If you do then you will ping when you go through customs and you will end up having to strip to your underwear to satisfy the curiosity of a rude Nazi with halitosis.)

Part 2: Getting to Know Paris

1. Getting orientated

Paris is like big sweet shop. Before you gorge yourself on the sherbet dip and find that you don't have any room left for a liquorice Catherine wheel, you need to look around and get your bearings. The best way to orientate yourself – and to, almost literally, obtain an overview of Paris – is to buy a ticket for one of the open-topped tourist buses such as Les Cars Rouge. Sit on the top of the bus with a map on your lap and follow your route all the way round. If you stay on the bus for a full circuit the round trip will take between two hours and two and a half hours.

(Incidentally, hotels give away quite decent maps sponsored by large stores but newsagents sell excellent red pocket-sized maps of Paris which are much better. They're about as thick as a normal paperback but smaller. Even the Parisians use them. They are more comprehensive, more durable and more portable than most tourist maps.)

When you climb aboard, the conductor will hand you a set of personal headphones which you can plug into the side of the bus. You can choose the language delivered to you and so listen to a running commentary describing the sights you are passing.

This is the quick and easy way to orientate yourself and to decide which bits of the city you really want to explore more thoroughly. When you've gone all the way round get off and have a coffee and then just get back on the bus (your ticket allows you to get on and off wherever and whenever you like for two days) and use the bus like an unusually convenient and inexpensive taxi. Despite having spent much of our lives in Paris we still do this quite regularly and find that the tourist bus makes quite a good taxi service.

2. Remember that Paris is a lived-in city

Unlike London, which is a city for businessmen, holiday-makers and shoppers, Paris is a city that millions of people really live in. They don't live in the suburbs, an hour's train ride out of town, they live in the city centre – often within walking distance of where they work, where they go to school, where they shop and where they meet friends. You'll see children going to school or the park, mothers and babies doing the grocery shopping and business people walking to work. Even those Parisians who have a cottage or a chateau in the country still consider themselves to be Parisian above all else.

Naturally, in order to cater for this large live-in population there are lots of 'proper' shops in the city centre: shops selling onions and vacuum cleaners rather than just providing tourists with hamburgers and silly T-shirts. Generally speaking (and excluding, for example, the shops selling the vacuum cleaners) the stores which cater for the Parisians are much more fun, and provide better value, than the shops which cater for tourists.

3. Enjoy café society

Paris is as famous for its cafés as it is for the Eiffel Tower. And, because of its cafés, Paris is the most rewarding city in the world for people watchers. Sitting in a café, at a table facing outwards, is probably the best way to enjoy this pastime.

If you're looking for a café with history, and you want to be able to say that you've probably sat at a table where famous American novelists or French existentialists have spilt their wine, then the seven best cafés still in existence are probably: Les Deux Magots, Lipp, Café de Flore, La Dôme, Café de La Paix, La Coupole and La Rhumerie. Inside Les Deux Magots there are plaques on a bench commemorating the fact that Jean-Paul Sartre and Simon de

—

—

—

Beauvoir 'sat there'. Aficionados of the Café de Flore will tell you that they spent a good deal of time there too. Sartre was a tourist sight in Paris in the 1960's and 1970's. He was arrested three times for distributing banned literature but never charged. As Charles de Gaulle remarked: 'One does not imprison Voltaire'. We once saw a French magazine article about Sartre which described him as Che Guevera with a pipe. Albert Camus also spent a lot of time in Les Deux Magots and the Café de Flore but we can't tell which seat he favoured. Maybe he just took pot luck. (If you return to Café de Flore try upstairs. It is supposed to be less fashionable but it has a special atmosphere of its own.)

These are among the most exciting and famous cafés in the world and have been for the best part of a century. London invented coffee houses but abandoned them. Today, only Vienna has cafés which match those of Paris.

Some tourists complain that the price for a coffee or a cup of tea in a famous Parisian café is high. Prices are quite high (though often not much worse than the price of a much less drinkable beverage in a motorway service station in Britain). But when people complain it is usually because they have made the mistake of assuming that they are just paying for the drink. They aren't. When you order a drink in a Parisian café (particularly a pavement café) you are renting a seat so that you can watch the passing show. And there you sit, in comfort, while pedestrians hurry past. And you can sit in judgement, too. Commenting on their clothes, their walk and their purchases. And if, perchance, it starts to rain you can sit smugly in the warm and dry while they struggle to put up their umbrellas and battle with the wind.

The famous cafés are good to visit but if you just want to have a drink, use the loo, eat or just watch the world totter by then almost any café you come across will do very nicely. There are more cafés in Paris than there are estate agents in the average British high street. It's difficult to walk more than a hundred yards in central Paris without passing a café and in some parts of the city the cafés seem to be breeding and out of control. It's sometimes hard to see how they all manage to stay in business. But they do and it isn't just the

tourists who keep the cafés alive. The Parisians regard cafés as an utterly essential part of their daily lives.

Look into a café in the early morning and you will see workmen in overalls standing side by side at the bar with businessmen in smart suits, all starting the day with a brandy or a glass of wine. They're fortifying themselves for the day ahead. They'll be there again in the evening, having a drink to fortify themselves for the journey home.

Incidentally, only gauche Americans call out 'Garcon!' when they want a waiter. (And some of them really do.) This is rude and stupid, for a waiter working in a café, bistro or restaurant in Paris is a skilled professional who expects to be called 'sir' ('Monsieur') and regards himself as being about on a social par with dentists, lawyers or senior civil servants. (The word 'bistro', by the way, comes with and without a 't' at the end.) Do not patronise a Parisian waiter, or treat him condescendingly, or you will wait a long time for your order to arrive. Even in the most modest establishment you should call the waiter 'Monsieur'. (The vast majority of waiters are male.) And, of course, only a fool complains about anything in a restaurant before they have eaten.

In cold weather the best drink to order is a vin chaud. (Pronounced 'van show'.) This is hot red wine. It should be served with a slice of lemon or orange, cinnamon and heaps of sugar. Vin chaud isn't always on the menu (especially in the posher places) but they always serve it because it's what the locals love to drink when the weather is cold. We have introduced the delights of a vin chaud to numerous friends. All now declare it to be their favourite way to consume alcohol.

While sitting in cafés we love watching Parisians park their cars. It's great fun. In Britain, if a driver comes along in a fifteen foot long car and finds a fourteen foot long space he will probably look at the space for a moment, curse loudly and then drive on. The British motorist looks for a space into which his car will fit. This isn't the French way. In Paris the driver makes the space fit his car, rather than the other way round. He will simply reverse into the space as hard as he can and bump the car behind back as far as it will go. This will usually mean that the car he has backed into will be shunted into the car behind it. And so on and so on. The driver will then nudge the car at the front of the space he wants to get into. And eventually he will get a fifteen foot long car into a fourteen foot space which he has turned into a fifteen and a half foot long space. The fun is repeated when a driver of one of the cars which has been shunted comes along and wants to move his car.

In Britain if a driver finds that he is sandwiched in by two cars whose bumpers touch his then he will probably jump up and down and start tearing out hair. In Paris the driver simply jumps into his car and reverses into the car behind and then shunts into the car in front until he has created enough space to enable him to drive out into the traffic. He will, of course, do this without signalling because signalling is cissy and not something the French do unless they intend to drive in a dead straight line and want to confuse the motorist travelling behind them.

We once saw a car on which the owner had tied the sort of floats boat owners use to protect their craft when moored. The floats were obviously there to provide some protection while the car was parked and they seemed to do the job well.

Sadly, you will notice that some clever Parisians have bought themselves extremely tiny Smart cars which are so short that they can be reversed up to the pavement and parked with the front of the car pointing directly outwards and towards the traffic. This is cheating since it deprives café-sitters of delightful entertainment, and we don't think it ought to be allowed.

If you want to enjoy the spectacle of watching the Parisians park (and unpark) their cars, make sure that you take a table which will give you a good view of a decent stretch of kerb. Cafés in streets linking into the Champs-Elysées are particularly good for this type of entertainment.

Finally, it is worth remembering that in addition to an apparently endless number of cafés, bistros and winebars, Paris also contains a number of excellent tea salons. Almost every arrondissement has one. Some entertain their customers with puppet shows or piano music while others merely concentrate on providing their customers with a vast variety of different teas from which to choose.

4. Know where to shop

Most visitors to Paris assume that the best shops are to be found on the Champs-Elysées. This is not true. The Champs-Elysées is a splendid thoroughfare which contains a number of excellent and traditional Parisian cafés (the best known among them being Fouquets – which can be found about half way up on the left hand side) but which contains more airline offices and car showrooms than decent shops. There are several arcades (the Lido arcade being by far the most interesting) and one or two spectacular megastores but you will find much better shops elsewhere in Paris.

The best big stores in Paris are Galeries Lafayette and Printemps, which are conveniently placed next to one another on the boulevard Haussemann, just behind the place de l'Opera. Third best is La Samaritaine which is situated just east of the Palais du Louvre. Of the three La Samaritaine is probably least likely to interest you if you are just visiting and most likely to interest you if you are looking for a duvet or a kettle. If you can't find what you are looking for in one of these three stores then you probably won't find it in central Paris. Outside these stores there are some excellent pavement stalls selling cheaper products – ties, scarves, watches and those peculiar kitchen implements which look so good when being demonstrated by an expert but which invariably prove unusable when you get them home.

Even if you don't want to purchase anything you really should visit Galeries Lafayette. There is nowhere in the world quite like it. The food and toy departments are particularly amazing. And for a breath taking moment, go into the main store, pass the counters selling perfumes and watches and look up. The inside of the store is a huge atrium which is, at Christmas time, filled with an enormous Christmas tree. Just how they get such a huge tree into the store is a mystery akin to the old ship in the bottle puzzle. If you're in Paris in the weeks before Christmas it is also well worth while taking a long look at the shop windows of Galeries Lafayette and Printemps. Both stores usually fill at least some of their windows with special displays for children. The stores even erect raised platforms so that small children don't have to be held up by their parents, but can stand

and watch the moving puppets and other toys. Galeries Lafayette usually has the best Christmas lights in the city.

The best fashion stores are to be found in the avenue Montaigne, and the city's best boutiques are found along the rue St Honoré. Whether you are looking for luggage, jewellery, stationery or a sandwich you'll find it along here.

We're delighted to report that small shops survive and thrive in Paris.

Four main forces have ruined Britain's town and city centres. First, the supermarkets whose buying power and pricing policies mean that thousands of small specialist shops have gone bankrupt. Secondly, the fast food restaurants which sell basic, fat-rich food so cheaply that bistros and cafés cannot compete. Thirdly, the local councils whose rate demands are exorbitant. And fourthly, the red tape produced by the Government.

Parisian shop keepers and café owners have survived these forces because French councils have kept rates down and because the French (often with the connivance of their Government) ignore those bits of European Union red tape which they don't like, or which they find unduly restrictive or inconvenient.

The short street where we live, which is by no means unusual, contains a mattress maker, a laundry, a plumbing supplies store, a greengrocer, an architect, a picture framer, a furniture restorer, four traditional cafés, an Internet café, an estate agent, a dress shop, a furniture store and heaven knows what else. All this despite the fact that there are half a dozen supermarkets within easy walking distance.

5. The best way to see Paris

Without a doubt, the best way to see Paris is to walk. Unlike many other capitals Paris is remarkably compact. Technically, the distance from the Eiffel Tower in the west to Sacre Coeur in the north is less than four miles (though in practice you should at least double that to allow for side-stepping other pedestrians and getting lost a few times en route). The 'official' distance from the Arc de Triomphe in the far west to the Bastille in the extreme East is the same. It is, remarkably, just over three miles from the Palais du Luxembourg in the south of the city to Sacre Coeur in the north. You can walk right across Paris in a day (though you might want to take a taxi back to your hotel if you do) and since those who control the city decided long ago to limit the number of skyscrapers to one (the Montparnasse tower) you can spot major landmarks such as the Eiffel Tower and Sacre Coeur from just about anywhere in the city. If we lose our bearings we use these iconic landmarks to help us find out where we are and how to get where we want to be if that isn't where we are. If you see what we mean. The general lack of skyscrapers casting unwanted, ugly shadows over the city also means that the famous Parisian light is still one of the city's best features.

For years one of our favourite pastimes in Paris has been to walk aimlessly, following only our inclinations and the sight of an interesting piece of architecture, a curious courtyard, an enticing park or a fascinating view. We walk until we manage to lose ourselves, strolling along boulevards and alleyways and through parks galore and then find our way back home without using the metro, a taxi or a map.

There are, incidentally, plenty of old-fashioned shoe repairers in Paris. Just keep an eye open as you walk around near your hotel and you'll probably soon find one. Alternatively, just ask at the hotel reception.

If you walk around Paris you will discover and see all sorts of things that are lost to those who travel everywhere by bus or taxi. The French even have a word for a person who wanders through Paris. They call him a flâneur – someone who strolls, saunters, or wanders the streets at random – looking for experiences rather than knowledge. The true flâneur will 's'arrêtant souvent pour regarder' (stop often to look).

6. Staying alive (coping with the traffic)

The one snag about getting around Paris on foot is the traffic. French motorists regard pedestrians as fair game and if you want to stay upright and avoid becoming a hood ornament on some battered Renault you must take great care when crossing even the smallest road. Some of the wider avenues require courage, timing and athleticism if you are to get from one side to the other in good condition. Timing is everything and you must, of course, always try to keep one hand free so that you can make rude gestures at motorists who whizz past you.

The most impossible roads to cross are the Champs-Elysées and the place de la Concorde. We firmly believe that there are nervous tourists on the island in the middle of the place de la Concorde who have been living there for decades; paralysed into immobility by the constant sea of speeding traffic whirling around them. Swimming through a shark-infested sea would be less of a challenge than crossing the place de la Concorde on foot. Motorists don't take much notice of the traffic lights around the rest of Paris but on the Champs-Elysées and the place de la Concorde, they do, fortunately, regard them with a little respect. And so wait for the moment and take it briskly. Don't ever be tempted to try to cross the ten lines of traffic which scream up and down the Champs-Elysées when the lights are against you. It will be the last mistake you make.

7. Ignore zebra crossings (motorists do)

Generally speaking, you should not be misled into thinking that the white strips of paint with which the city has decorated the roads at various points bear any resemblance to zebra crossings, or are of any value to pedestrians.

The curious idea of allowing pedestrians to cross roads in safety at certain points was introduced by the Germans when they invaded France during the Second World War. The Germans were appalled at the messy way the French just wandered across roads whenever the fancy took them. Sadly, of course, the French never like being told what to do and they particularly dislike being told what to do by Germans whom they generally regard as bullet-headed bullies with no sense of style, no sense of taste and an appallingly childish sense of humour. Consequently, motorists treat these crossings with utter disdain; often making them utterly unusable by parking right across them.

French zebra crossings look much the same as zebra crossings in

Britain (without the Belisha beacons) but you must not allow this to confuse you. The white strips of paint across the road have absolutely no relevance and should be regarded as artistic interventions rather than as invitations to cross the road safely.

8. Watch out for motorbikes
It is vital to watch out for the mad motorcyclists who race through Paris on unusually noisy machines. They usually do this in the middle of the night so that they can wake up as many people as possible but occasionally they race around during the daytime to knock over a few pedestrians.

9. Buy a ladder
There is one way for a pedestrian to cross Parisian roads without difficulty. We found it by accident when we were decorating our apartment and had to buy a ladder.

We found that walking through Paris with a full-length aluminium ladder enabled us to get through the traffic without any trouble. Whenever we wanted to cross the road the traffic stopped for us straight away.

Of course, you may find that there is a limited amount of space available in your hotel room for storing the ladders you purchase each day.

10. When frogs become toads
When they get behind the wheel of a car the French all behave like Mr Toad. Female French motorists behave like Mrs Toad. (For the record, female drivers in France are even worse than the men. Some say that French, female drivers are even more stupid and more arrogant than Belgian motorists.)

When French drivers get into a car they are only interested in three things: the accelerator pedal, the ashtray and the horn. The first and third of these they press all the time. The second, they fill as quickly as possible.

A French friend of ours, who has lived in Paris all her life, claims that French drivers need three hands; one for their cigarette, one to fondle the knee of any accompanying passenger, and one to make rude gestures to other drivers and pedestrians and to make the sign of the cross after close calls.

How do they steer? With their knees, of course.

Regardless of the size or age of their car, drivers in Paris take it for granted that they are more important than all other motorists and are, therefore, always entitled to assume that they have the right of way. So, for example, if there is a crossing ahead they will assume that approaching traffic will give way to them. This wouldn't be a problem if the drivers in the approaching traffic hadn't made exactly the same assumption.

Parisian motorists regard traffic congestion as a personal affront because it stops them driving fast and showing how well they can handle a car when it only has two wheels on the ground.

Traffic rules are seen as interesting suggestions which drivers will consider if they aren't too busy. Road signs which demand some sort of action are regarded as a clear threat to the motorist's intellectual freedom and personal liberty to do what he wants to do when he wants to do it.

It is our considered view that the primary aim of all Parisian motorists is not to arrive at a destination but to kill, maim or simply terrify as many pedestrians as possible. And to a French motorist a destination is simply somewhere that they reach before they turn around and do it all again.

All this means that the safest way to cross the road in Paris is to assume that every motorist you see is deliberately trying to kill you. It is just possible that one or two of them may not be, but this is the safest way to deal with things.

N.B. Readers who have seen films such as *Ronin* and *The Bourne Identity* will have some idea of the way the French drive. It is generally assumed by people who don't know Paris very well that these films were shot using stunt drivers. We believe that this is a myth and that the films were made in ordinary rush hour traffic.

11. Traffic jams

Traffic jams aren't as bad in Paris as they are in London or other

British cities. This is because French drivers tend to nudge each other out of the way, rather as dodgem drivers push aside inconveniently parked dodgem cars. No French driver would sit in his stationary car for ten minutes let alone for a period of several hours.

Nevertheless, there are some jams, particularly at peak times, and the French moan that traffic delays have interfered badly with the time they have available to conduct affairs of the heart.

Having an affair used to be known as having a 'cinq à sept' (5 p.m. to 7 p.m.) because that was when a husband saw his mistress or a wife saw her lover.

However, the traffic in Paris at that time of the day is now bad. Take thirty minutes travelling time out of a 'cinq à sept' and you are left with the sort of romantic sprint no Frenchman (or Frenchwoman) would willingly accept.

12. Pollution control

The Parisians have found a simple but effective way to deal with pollution caused by cars. They monitor pollution levels and if these reach unacceptable levels then half the cars which normally enter Paris are banned for a day. The authorities do this by banning cars according to whether their number plate ends with an even or an odd number.

The very rich get round this by having one car with an even number and one car with an odd number.

13. Motorcades with police escorts

In most cities around the world you can be pretty sure that if you see a motorcade coming there will be at least one famous and very important person sitting in one of the cars.

This is not the case in France.

A few years ago, when France was in what French economists now like to dismiss as 'a bit of a temporary cash flow crisis', the nation applied for a loan. In order to decide whether or not to make the loan, the institution to which they had applied sent some economists over to Paris to take a look at the books and see what security the French could offer. Not wanting to attract attention to their financial predicament the French sent a mini bus to the airport to pick up the economists but deliberately didn't send a police escort. Inevitably, and perhaps predictably, the mini bus full of economists got stuck in heavy traffic. This did not go down well with the economists who were allegedly rather peeved at being forced to spend several hours in a queue with ordinary people. The French Government's application for a loan was refused.

As a result of that unfortunate incident the French Government now gives a full police escort to anyone who might be in a position to cause even the slightest embarrassment to France. Red lights and pedestrians are all ignored.

If you see a limousine being escorted through London by a squad of outriders and a line of police cars you can be pretty sure that the limousine contains either a member of the Royal Family or the Prime Minister's wife. But if you see a limousine being escorted through Paris the chances are that the vehicle contains a team of Polish mining engineers, a platoon of Venezuelan oil drillers or a group of representatives from the International Olympic Committee investigating the possibility of allowing Paris to host the Olympics in 2064.

The Parisians are, of course, less respectful towards these visitors than is their Government. We once watched in astonishment as a cavalcade of cars, which was screaming through Paris and accompanied by the usual motorcyclists with flashing blue lights, was booed and jeered by just about every pedestrian wandering along. The boos and jeers raced along the pavement at the same speed as the cars and the passengers inside must have realised that, despite their escort, they were not welcome in the city. We bought a local paper and discovered that the cars contained representatives of a Chinese trade mission. The Parisians, knowing the identity of the cars' occupants, were taking advantage of the opportunity to show their feelings about the Chinese political system.

14. Nevertheless, walking is best
Despite all this, there is no doubt that the best way to see Paris is to walk. Pedestrians see so many things that others do not notice:

enticing alleyways, exquisite courtyards, beautiful doors (perhaps the most attractive doorway in Paris adorns an exquisitely ornate apartment building in the avenue Rapp) and beautifully dressed shop windows. There is even a building on the quai Branly which has plants, grasses, ferns and mosses covering its exterior.

15. French notaires

As you wander, keep an eye open for any door which has two large gold disks attached to the wall above it in such a way that the disks can be seen by pedestrians approaching from either direction. When you see these gold disks (which contain the figure of Justice, sitting above the words Republique Française) you will know that a notaire works in the building. Notaires are French lawyers who deal with all the nation's official paperwork. Much of their work involves the buying and selling of property. A single notaire often acts for both the buyer and the seller because he is paid not to represent one party's interests but to make sure that the whole thing is done according to the law. Many notaires act as estate agents too. Fortunately, the French trust their notaires in a way that we don't trust our lawyers or our estate agents. The notaire who strays from the path of righteousness faces severe penalties.

16. Pedalling through Paris

The French cycle around Paris a good deal and there are cycle lanes criss-crossing the city. You can now get almost anywhere in the city of Paris in the comparative safety of a specially designated cycle lane. Bicycles can be hired by the day or the week. Your hotel should be able to help you find a bicycle rental agency.

Where cycle lanes haven't been designated, or run close to the traffic, French cyclists who find the idea of entrusting their lives to the sobriety and good manners of French motorists will often cycle on the pavement. You, being an honest and responsible citizen would not naturally dream of doing such a thing.

A popular modern alternative to the bicycle is the small, folding, aluminium scooter. In most of the rest of the world the enthusiasm for these gadgets lasted about as long as a piece of Gerald Ratner's cheap jewellery might have been expected to survive but scooters live on in Paris. We have even seen sophisticated looking businessmen using them to whizz from one business appointment to another. It's quite startling to see a perfectly groomed Parisian businessman scooting along the pavement with his briefcase under his arm, his pink lambswool scarf flung, with inborn Gallic casual skill, over his left shoulder and his 100 euro haircut moving lightly in the self-generated breeze. (No other nation has so many words for scarf and no other country has an entire culture built around different ways to tie a scarf.)

Small, mini-wheeled motorised scooters (fitted with quite powerful engines) are also popular. These produce as much noise as a Formula One racing car and reach terrifying speeds. The riders usually appear to be students, though they whizz past so quickly that it is difficult to tell.

17. Le Metro: The French underground
Do not confuse the Paris Metro with the London Underground. The former is useful, fast, efficient and relatively clean.

Finding your way around Paris with the aid of the Metro isn't difficult once you understand that the Parisians refer to the Metro lines according to the name of the station at the end of the line. This makes picking out a route a bit like doing one of those maze puzzles which are published in children's comics.

Most Metro stations are equipped with large, electrically lit maps so that you can press two buttons and check out your route. Unfortunately, although theoretically very useful, these maps are usually commandeered by English schoolchildren who, being accustomed to getting their entertainment by pressing buttons, are unwilling to allow themselves to be torn away from the entertainment. It is, therefore, usually best to obtain a small map and to plan your route before you go down underground.

Once you know where you want to go buy a carnet of ten tickets (unless you know that you won't ever use that many). This is cheaper and saves time. You must keep your ticket once you are on the train because occasionally inspectors come round. They are empowered to do terrible things to people who are travelling without having paid the proper fare. We find that used Metro tickets make quite good book marks.

The white-tiled corridors which connect Metro stations are usually neat and clean and some of the best musicians in Paris work in them. The stations themselves are often lavishly and imaginatively decorated. They are also imaginatively named and provide a remarkable history lesson of statesmen, artists, battles, financiers, writers, and artists. Well-known individuals commemorated as Metro stations include Charles de Gaulle, Franklin D Roosevelt, George V, Garibaldi, Bolivar, Victor Hugo, Emile Zola, Lamarck, Anatole France and Robespierre. Less well known today, but still remembered as Metro stations, are Felix Faure (a French politician who died at his desk with his mistress on his lap – chunks of her hair had to be cut off to release his fingers), Guy Moquet (a student shot by the Germans in 1941), Père Lachaise (who founded a convent where the cemetery bearing his name now stands), Hoche (a general in the Republican army who began life as a stable boy) and Motte Picquet (a naval general of the American War of Independence). The Metro station Abbesses is named after the 16 abbesses of an order created in 1133 by Louis VI. The stations Stalingrad, Austerlitz and Wagram were named after Napoleonic battles. (Don't look for Waterloo. That's in London.) Look around inside the Metro stations and you'll find all sorts of curiosities.

When you reach your destination and want to get off the train you must open the door yourself. If you fail to do this and no one else is getting off at your stop you will be stuck on the train.

Seats near to the doors are reserved for the war wounded and for pregnant women. Anyone who is both war wounded and pregnant is, presumably, entitled to two seats.

(Pregnant women are also entitled to go to the front of queues just about everywhere, though this is not a privilege that it is wise to exploit if you do not have a discernible bump. Some pregnant women also claim that they are entitled to cross roads wherever they like. A pregnant friend of ours tried this out. Once.)

Sadly and embarrassingly, the only really bad behaviour we have seen on the Metro came from British schoolchildren on a trip to Paris. The accompanying schoolteachers seemed utterly unconcerned about the chaos and disorder their pupils were causing. We could only conclude that the pupils were attending a school for putative football hooligans. We obtained little comfort from the knowledge that Britain's reputation as the world's leading source of hooligans is in safe hands.

18. L'Autobus

There are loads of buses in Paris and you can get on a bus using the same tickets that you've bought for use on the Metro. We are reliably informed that all these buses go somewhere, though it isn't always easy to work out just where they are going or when they are likely to get there. We use buses occasionally. We get on one if it seems to be going in the right direction and we then get off if it appears to have veered from its course or if it has become too crowded. This pragmatic approach works well for us.

Occasionally, passengers on a bus will start lengthy arguments with the driver. When this happens it is wise to leave the bus immediately. We once stood on a stationary bus for forty five minutes while a group of passengers and the driver argued heatedly and with great vigour. We had some difficulty following the argument but we gathered that the dispute had started because the bus had arrived at its stop three minutes late. It did not seem to occur to anyone that the bus would have arrived at its destination forty five minutes earlier if the dispute about tardiness had been postponed. There is no point in trying to explain things like this to the French. Their love of a loud argument is far greater than their love of logic or, indeed, their love of getting to their destination on time.

19. Travelling by taxi

French taxis look like private cars though they do have lights of varying sizes fitted to their roofs. Even Parisians find it difficult to decide whether a taxi is available or not, and stopping one in the street is nowhere near as easy as it is London. Sitting in the comfort of a pavement café we have often been entertained by the sight of fur-coated women with large packages from Christian Dior and Louis Vuitton jumping up and down on the pavement as they struggle, vainly, to attract the attention of taxi drivers.

Queuing at a taxi rank is a relatively sure way to find a taxi but unfortunately the concept of queuing (particularly when it involves standing outside in the cold) is not something with which the Parisians feel entirely comfortable. If you're in a queue anywhere other than at a mainline railway station (where there are steel barriers to keep the queues neatly defined, and special taxi captains to decide which queue member gets into which taxi) you will have to keep a close eye on the people behind you and, indeed, on the other side of the street. Once a taxi arrives, get into it quickly. Don't stand around on the pavement saying 'After you' and 'No, after you' or telling the driver where you want to go. On more than one occasion we have lost our taxi to a woman who has rushed across the street and dived in through the door on the other side of the vehicle. It hasn't always been the same woman who has done this but it has always been a woman.

The best and most efficient way to get a taxi is to go back to your hotel and telephone for one. If you are several miles away at the time you will, of course, have to get to your hotel by Metro, by bus or on foot. The hotel receptionist or concierge will have suitable telephone numbers and should, if you ask nicely, make the call for you. There is, as you will have doubtless already noticed, a snag: you can only do this when you are already in your hotel and going out and not when you are out and trying to get back.

If you have a mobile phone with you, and you have the number of a taxi firm and the courage to call them up all by yourself, then you can ring for a taxi wherever you are in the city. The taxi firm employees who answer the telephone usually speak English though they may not admit this to you, particularly if they think that English is the only language you speak. The French get great pleasure out of treating all foreigners as deaf lunatics and this is easier to do when they have the language advantage. If you don't have a mobile telephone you can try using a call box and we wish you luck in your endeavours.

Secrets of Paris

Theoretically, passengers are not allowed in the front seat of an ordinary taxi (mainly, we suspect, because that is where the driver keeps his maps, his cigarettes, his cigarette butts, his baguette sandwich and his copy of *Le Soir*) and so if more than three of you wish to ride together you will, theoretically, have to order a limousine or one of those ugly monstrosities known as a People Carrier. Alternatively, and at far less expense, you can simply bribe the taxi driver by giving him a 20 euro note before you all get in. You could try something smaller but be prepared to make a run for it if the driver decides to be offended by such a small bribe.

French taxi drivers are not terribly well-informed about their city. Unlike their London counterparts, who have to learn 'the knowledge' before they can drive cabs in the city centre, we suspect that anyone with a driving licence and access to a motor vehicle of some kind can become a taxi driver in Paris. In addition most Parisian taxi drivers have an unusually poorly developed sense of direction and rely on a satellite navigation system, a map spread out on the front passenger seat beside them and the fact that Paris is a small city and so if they keep riding round and round they will eventually arrive somewhere close to where you want to be.

Parisian taxi drivers are also utterly useless at avoiding traffic jams or demonstrations – even when they know in advance where the problem areas are likely to be. Indeed, we suspect that the love of demonstrations among the French in general is so well-developed in the city that taxi drivers deliberately make their way towards the nearest blockage, just as a lemming might head for the nearest cliff. And, as always, there is a risk that if a taxi driver thinks you are foreign he may take you twice round the city even if your proposed journey is quite a short one. As a general rule we always make fuss if we find ourselves passing the Eiffel Tower more than twice in a single journey.

We have yet to meet a Parisian taxi driver who has the sort of pride in his work commonly found among London cabbies. The only upside is that Parisian taxi drivers are, generally speaking, taciturn and rather gloomy individuals who, unlike their opinionated British counterparts, are not greatly interested in discussing the shortcomings of their Government.

20. Finding specific buildings

When streets in Paris run parallel to the river Seine the numbers of the buildings generally follow the direction in which the river is flowing. When streets run perpendicular to the river, building numbers begin at the end nearest the river. Even numbered buildings are on the right hand side of the street or avenue, and odd numbered buildings are on the left.

21. A boring note about electrical appliances

The French use a different type of electricity. This may be because they get most of their electricity from nuclear power plants or, more probably, because French electricity contains more fat, alcohol and nicotine.

Whatever the cause of the difference the fact is that in our experience you may have some slight difficulty making English appliances function effectively in France. Sockets and plugs for telephones, computers and other electrical appliances are, of course, utterly different to the ones used in the United Kingdom. Some electrical appliances and chargers simply won't adapt and work in France. Or, rather, they may well work for a while before catching fire and blowing up. (All of this should provide great comfort to eurosceptics. The EU's aim for a United States of Europe will never reach fruition until we all start using the same sort of electricity.)

We have no practical advice for you concerning any of this. But we thought you should know.

22. Beggars: a major growth industry

Like most major European cities Paris has, in recent years, become infested with beggars. Most come from Eastern Europe and are en route to Britain where they know that the State supplies beggars with five bedroomed houses, new cars and dishwashers. In France the State is less generous, unless you happen to be a State employee, and so beggars tend to congregate around well-known tourist areas which are, as a result, now just about as hazardous as the entrance to the Bazaar in Istanbul. The most annoying are the teams of young girls who target the main railway stations, the parks and the boulevards near to the big cafés and the main shops. The police do their best to move them on and stop them becoming too much of a nuisance but, sadly, their success in this endeavour is, at best, mixed. The beggars know that while they won't get much from the French the British are the softest touch in the world. The beggar's first words will usually be 'Do you speak English?'. If you admit that you do the beggar will thrust a small scruffy piece of paper into your hand explaining why you should immediately hand over a decent chunk of your holiday money. If the girl doing the begging doesn't have a baby in her arms the note will tell you that there is a baby nearby starving and desperately needing sustenance. (The note won't mention the thug sitting in the café round the corner, sipping wine, smoking cigarettes and reading the paper. It is, of course, to him that your money will go.) You may feel (as we used to) that a small donation is a small price to pay for a guilt free conscience. Try hard not to succumb to temptation. You will, in the end, find the guilt much easier to live with. The modern East European beggar doesn't accept a single euro coin with a smile and a nod. She will regard a donation not as a sign of generosity but as a sign of weakness to be exploited. Once you've handed over one coin you will be followed wherever you go by the recipient of your largesse demanding more extensive funding. Worse still, she will probably call over her confederates and so you will soon be surrounded by impatient and remarkably persistent supplicants – all wanting food for their starving babies. Eager fingers will pull at your luggage and your clothes and (if within reach) your wallet.

We once sat on a bench in a park and watched an English couple give money to one of these beggars. Once they had done this the beggar became quite belligerent and demanded more coins. When the couple shook their heads the beggar simply snatched the ice cream the man had just started eating and ran off with it laughing. She and her friends then shared it.

Incidentally, beggars should not be confused with tramps. Paris has always had its clochards (tramps). Most live on the river bank (traditionally under the bridges). They don't usually ask for money and they are not a nuisance to visitors to the city.

23. Parisian street entertainers

For a while at the end of the 20th century and start of the 21st the most popular occupation in Paris seemed to be dressing up, standing still and pretending to be someone (or something else). There were several editions of Charlie Chaplin, countless versions of the Statue of Liberty (complete with flaming torch), at least one Tutankhamen (we were never quite sure whether the variations we saw in different parts of Paris were the same person dressed up or different people dressed up) and numerous mummies.

The human statues seem to have more or less disappeared (though, given the vagaries of popular fashions in the world of entertainment, they will undoubtedly make a come back eventually).

The disappearance of the statues does not mean, however, that Paris is devoid of street entertainers. Far from it. The pavements of the City of Light sometimes seem to be positively awash with men and women earning a living through their talents in the wide ranging world of show business.

Still quite popular, for example, are the street entertainers who make their living on the pavements outside the big cafés and who earn their money by following tourists and mimicking their walk. They do this to amuse the café patrons and can be quite cruel. We've sat in cafés for hours, not brave enough to move lest we find ourselves mimicked as we leave.

And there are masses of street musicians in Paris too. In addition to solo guitarists it is not at all unusual to see groups, bands and even orchestras performing in streets, squares and parks. We have, on several occasions, seen an entire orchestra busking in the open air.

24. Confidence tricksters

Paris, like all big cities, is full of confidence tricksters, though in France they do tend to do things with a certain amount of style. The most famous con man who worked in Paris was the fellow who made a good living out of selling the Eiffel Tower to rich Americans. He told them it was being demolished and that the French Government wanted to sell it for scrap. A co-conspirator who worked in a French Government office helped by providing an office where the banker's drafts could be handed over.

Sadly, you're more likely to come across grifters working simple short cons.

Here are one or two of the ones we've come across (either because they've happened to us or because we've seen them happen to other people).

1. A nice young couple gave their camera to a stranger so that he could take picture of them in front of the Eiffel Tower. He backed away to get them into shot and then turned and ran off with their camera.

2. There is a man in Paris who wanders around the public parks with a fake identity card slung around his neck and a pocket full of tickets. He approaches people sitting on benches or chairs and sells them tickets. We've seen him in several different parks. He is careful to hit only on tourists since the Parisians and locals know that there is no charge to sit on benches and ordinary chairs in local parks. (There may, however, be a charge to sit on deck chairs.)

3. We were walking along a street near our apartment when we saw an expensive looking ring glittering on the pavement in front of us. Just before we got to it a smartly dressed man appeared from behind a car and picked it up. He then looked up, and seemed surprised to see us there. He held up the ring to show it to us. We looked at it and nodded. He tried it on. It did not fit any of his fingers. 'It ees losted,' he told us. We nodded our understanding and agreement. He tried to hand the ring to us. 'You take,' he said. 'It ees gold.' 'Oh no, we couldn't,' we said. 'We must take it to the police station.' 'No, no, no,' he said, shaking his head. 'You take.' He thrust the ring at us. Reluctantly, we took it, wondering how long it would take us to walk to the nearest police station and make a report. He smiled and nodded and started to walk away. Then, as though remembering something, he turned back. 'You give me money for food,' he said. 'Twenty euros. You have the ring.' We gave him the ring. At first he didn't want to take it. 'You keep the ring and give me money.' We said we would rather he kept the ring. He seemed disappointed

but when he realised that we were serious about not giving him money he took the ring and walked away. We followed discreetly, at a distance. In the next street we watched him drop the ring on the pavement and hide behind a car. The ring was brass. He probably had a pocket full of them.

25. Eating out

If you want to eat out in Paris please ignore the hamburger chains (of which there are now, sadly, quite a few in Paris) and choose instead the local speciality a 'croque monsieur' (ham and cheese on toast), 'croque madame' (a 'croque monsieur' with fried egg on top) or a 'croque végétarien' (toast with just the melted cheese). The hamburger bars are largely kept in business by travelling Britons and Americans and whatever we think of the French we owe them a chance to rid their country of these beastly places.

The words Le Menu means the set meal of the day (usually two or three courses and a drink at a fixed price). The words 'table d'hôte' officially means that the table is presided over personally by the host and hostess and is derived from the word d'hôtel. (In French the word 'hôtel' means a house, not somewhere for travellers to stay.)

If you're looking down the printed menu for something to select we suggest that you look for 'crudités' (a plateful of beautifully prepared and tasty raw vegetables – usually including tomato, beetroot, carrots and so on) and 'frites' (a vast plate full of chips). Together the two make a splendid meal and will nearly always be served with slices from a baguette (a long thin loaf which tastes absolutely nothing like the rubbish sold in British supermarkets). If you want to drink wine and don't know what to choose you could try 'vin de table du patron' (an ordinary wine recommended by the owner) or 'un ballon de rouge' (a glass of red wine).

26. Public lavatories

All travellers know the pain of needing a lavatory in a strange city. Once the need makes itself felt your every move and every gaze is governed by the search for relief. It is a quest that becomes as dedicated as a pilgrimage and as vital as a hunt for a matching blood donor. Each small building you spy becomes a target for your attention and you constantly rush from one side of the street to the other, each time thinking that you've found what you are looking for.

When you don't find anywhere you take advantage of the fact that in Paris every other building is a restaurant or a hotel or a café and you pop inside to take advantage of their lavatory. Being a hesitant and shy tourist you don't like to use the loo without buying something so you order a cup of coffee on your way down the stairs. When you go down the stairs, with your bladder full, you are determined that you'll leave the coffee untouched. But when you come back up the stairs, with your bladder empty, your resolve has weakened and it seems a pity to waste the coffee so you don't.

Half an hour later the whole business starts again. By the end of the day you've done nothing but search for lavatories and seen nothing but the insides of a hundred small cafés. That evening when you return to your hotel you take a solemn oath that tomorrow will be different, but when you start your day with rolls and coffee you doom yourself to another identical day of torment. When you finally leave and get back home and people ask you if you enjoyed the catacombs or the Champs-Elysées you lie and say, of course you did. They lie too and say how wonderful it all is. And so the secret life of the typical tourist remains a secret life.

The cafés in Paris are a godsend because they all have loos. (Usually either downstairs or upstairs.) Look for the word 'toilettes'. Men and woman sometimes have to share facilities. In rough parts of the city you may still come across one of the old hole-in-the-ground loos (called Turkish so as to blame some other country). If you come across one of these make sure that you are ready to leave before you press the flush button. And then move quickly if you want to avoid getting wet feet.

Some of the smarter Parisian cafés still have a woman sitting down in the lavatory section. She will have a little table beside her on which there will be a small bowl. You are supposed to put coins into the bowl if you use the loo. If you don't do this she will chase you for several miles through Paris hurling obscenities at your back. Never have we felt quite so ashamed of our country as when we once saw a teacher tell a crowd of English schoolchildren to go into a bar to use the loo, and to run in and out to avoid paying the 30 centime fee.

There are lady attendants looking after the 'official' loos too. For a small fee you get a clean lavatory, a towel, and soap. These women are professionals and they run their lavatories as a business. They deserve to make a fine living.

Finally, there are now in some areas of Paris the very latest high tech lavatories. Read the instructions, put your coin in and get in and out as quickly as you can. Those who have been caught in one of these loos during the cleansing process have been in no state to describe how bad it was afterwards.

27. Tipping

When artist Andy Warhol was shot, and thought to be dying, he was put into an ambulance with a friend who had also been shot. As they were about to drive off to the hospital the ambulance driver turned to Warhol's friend and said: 'If we sound the siren, it'll cost five dollars extra'.

That happened in New York, of course. And the French aren't quite as openly greedy as the Americans. They do, however, like a good tip and few people in the service industry in France do anything much without expecting a bonus; a little something on top of their salary, wage, fee or bill.

Working out just what to give isn't easy. If you give too little the recipient will regard you with utter contempt. If, on the other hand, you give too much the recipient will regard you with utter contempt. The right amount to tip is something between 10% and 20%, depending upon the quality of the service you have been given. Do not, however, make the mistake made by a rather particular friend of ours from Switzerland who spent two weeks in Paris carefully working out every tip with a calculator to make sure that he gave exactly 15% and not a centime more or less to everyone he met. His tipping was exemplary but he would have had more fun working for a fortnight in an accountant's office.

If the tip is automatically added to the bill (as it usually will be) it is customary to leave any small coins that you receive for the waiter to collect.

Part 3: Understanding France And The French

1. Introduction

There are people of many nationalities in Paris, but most of the people you'll bump into will probably be French. It is, therefore, necessary to know a little about them.

The French are not like us.

Generally speaking the French are greedy, vain, mean and selfish. 'Fais ce que tu veux' (do what you want) is a French family motto. The French are so full of self-regard that they don't give a fig about how others see them. 'I want to come back in another life as a Parisian; shallow, superficial, vain, self-obsessed, beautifully dressed, shopping, eating, talking rubbish for hours in smoky cafés,' wrote a correspondent recently.

These are not, however, attributes which the average Frenchman (were there such a creature) would regard as a sign of a character deficiency.

To understand the French you must realise that, in their eyes, members of every other nationality in the world are, by the very fact of not being French, labouring under a huge and unassailable disadvantage in the daily stroll through life. The French are the most politically incorrect, selfish people in the world. They are racist, xenophobic and chauvinistic and proud of it. They would not vote for anyone who was not at least some and preferably all of these things.

In recent years the British have been taught to disapprove of eccentricity and to try to eradicate it. The French, on the other hand, still respect eccentricity as exhibiting the very essence of individuality.

As a result of all this Paris is the least restricting city on the planet. It is a city where liberté, égalité and fraternité (freedom, equality and brotherhood) still mean something. It is a city where the will of the people is respected as in no other city on earth. So, for example, when a group of keen rollerbladers started rolling through the streets of Paris on Friday evenings the Mayor responded quickly not by banning the impromptu event (as we suspect the Mayor might have done in London) but by providing a police escort to make sure that rollerbladers weren't injured and motorists weren't too inconvenienced. In Paris the aim of the city politicians is to give the people what they want, whenever and however this is possible – however eccentric the demands might be. This is a pleasant contrast to the UK where politicians seem to prefer to spend public money stopping people doing things they want to do.

This section of *Secrets of Paris* is designed to introduce you to the French. There are, after all, so many of them living in Paris that it is difficult to avoid them completely. A modest understanding of what makes them tick and what makes them tock will help make your stay in their city more enjoyable.

2. The Parisians love Paris

The Parisians love their city. Many prefer to live there in cramped apartments rather than move out and live in relative luxury in the suburbs or in the countryside. You can buy a chateau with its own lake and parkland for the price of a small apartment in the centre of Paris but, although the French think of themselves as countrymen, not many of Parisians actually want to live too far away from their favourite cafés and restaurants.

Because of the high price of real estate in Paris many Parisians live in tiny, dark one or two room apartments which have no view and very little light. One bright and sunny afternoon we saw a respectably dressed old woman looking at her reflection in a shop window and using tweezers to pull hairs out of her chin. This puzzled us for a while until we realised that she was probably performing this rather private chore outside in the sunshine because her apartment was so dark that she would not have been able to see what she was doing in there.

Despite their love for Paris the Parisians are unbelievably blasé about their city. If you're lost or bewildered don't bother asking Parisians for help. An amazingly high percentage of Parisians have never visited the Hôtel des Invalides, been up the Eiffel Tower or gazed at Notre Dame cathedral. Because these things are always there they never bother with them. We have met visitors who have, after three days in Paris, seen more of the city's landmarks than Parisians who have lived there for a lifetime.

3. The male French attitude towards women

Women in France are idolised. French men love women and love French women most of all. And French women love themselves. But none of this alters the fact that France is very much a society dominated by men and run for men. Those who doubt this might like to remember that French women only got the vote in 1945 and up until 1965 a man could forbid his wife to go to work if he wanted her to stay at home.

4. The French love flowers

Paris is full of florists. Having flowers in abundance in the parks isn't enough for the Parisians. They want them in their homes too. There are more shops and markets selling flowers than in any other city we know. There are, for example, more than half a dozen excellent florists within hailing distance of our apartment. Naturally, the competition helps keep down the prices. You can buy anything common and most things rare. The best flower markets are the huge Marché aux Fleurs (which is close to Notre Dame) and the stalls next to La Madelaine where, the last time we looked, one of the market stall holders had put up a sign saying 'prière de toucher avec les yeux' (please touch with your eyes).

The florists are always busy because the French buy flowers for one another (as a 'cadeau') and for themselves ('pour la maison'). If you buy flowers for yourself the florist will cut and trim and wrap them nicely and give you advice about how much water you should give them and how often. (One florist once told us that tulips are gourmands, a thought which we rather liked.) If you tell the florist that the flowers are a present he or she will turn into an artist and cut and trim and wrap your selection in swathes of paper, clear cellophane and colourful ribbon and create an instant bouquet at no extra charge.

To the French (and, in particular, to the Parisians) luxuries are not things you don't need, don't want and can't afford. Luxury is an attitude and luxuries, such as flowers, are essentials which must be purchased before all else.

5. The French don't like Americans

To be honest, the French don't like anyone very much (not even other French people). But it is the Americans the French loathe most of all. Their disapproval of other nationalities is often tinged with some affection (their hatred of the English is softened with respect and regard for the old enemy) but the brand of hatred and contempt they feel for Americans is undiluted. When there is talk of yet another 'American offensive' somewhere in the world the French think that the journalist has simply forgotten to put the word 'are' in the middle of the phrase.

There are many things that the French don't like about Americans. For one thing they do not understand why Americans dress like golfers even when they are not playing golf. And for another they do not understand why Americans think they have the right to be rude to everyone they meet. There are without doubt many polite, courteous and self-effacing Americans (and we have met, and continue to enjoy the friendship of several) but, in general, the polite, gentle Americans don't travel much further than Idaho.

The French are rude, of course, but their defence is that they have given the world great literature, great art, great architecture, great food, great wine and Napoleon, the world's greatest man. The

French are obsessed with the arts and with literature. In a café a little while ago we found sugar cubes which had quotes from famous poets printed on the paper wrapping. What, demand the French, has America ever produced? Le Coca Cola, le hamburger and an endless series of films ripping off the French cinema. The French say that American rudeness comes because Americans regard possessions and wealth as the only things that matter. French rudeness, on the other hand, comes from a difficult to define sense of status which is based on the fact that there are no humble people and no humble jobs in France.

If you talk to the French they will explain the differences between the way they see the British and the way they see the Americans. They say that the British tend to apologise a great deal and to speak schoolboy French with great hesitancy. The Americans, on the other hand, shout and swagger a great deal and hardly ever bother to learn even the French for 'please', 'thank you', and 'get out of my way you miserable garlic eating little foreigner'. The British are gentle and modest. Americans are aggressive and arrogant and assume that they must always come first.

If you live in Paris for a while you'll soon see what the French mean. The other day, for example, we watched in absolute horror as a huge gang of Americans on bicycles rode through a quiet street in Paris. The Americans took up the entire road, blocking all the traffic and ignoring the traffic lights. They shouted abuse at pedestrians and motorists and, in general, behaved rather like a conquering army. This is by no means unusual behaviour for Americans in Paris and consequently it's hardly surprising that the Parisians dislike them.

We once stood on a bus in Paris and watched in amazement as a quartet of American tourists demanded that the bus driver take them to their hotel in Montmartre, which is, of course, where they wanted to go, rather than to the place de la Bastille, which is where the bus was supposed to go.

And we once sat in a café and listened in horror as a family of Americans demanded a thanksgiving dinner. When the French waiter made it clear (with some very eloquent French shrugging) that he didn't know (or care) what thanksgiving was, the Americans became quite hysterical and extremely aggressive. It didn't occur to them that the French might not celebrate their special holidays.

Here are four true stories which best illustrate the way the French regard the Americans.

First, in the 1991 Gulf War the French were pressured to show solidarity with the American invasion of Iraq. So they sent an aircraft carrier. The French politicians did not, however, want to upset their own internal Muslim population so they did not put any aircraft on the ship. That's diplomacy French style.

Second, a friend claims he once overheard this exchange between an American visitor and a custodian in the military museum at the Hôtel des Invalides. The American saw two skulls in a glass case but could not read the information card which was only in French.

'Whose are those skulls?' the American demanded, rather rudely.

'They belonged to Napoleon,' replied the custodian.

'Both of them?' demanded the American.

'Yes,' replied the custodian. 'The small one was when he was a boy and the big one when he was a man.'

'Oh,' said the American, nodding wisely.

Third, a young French friend of ours (a television executive, married to a high flying civil servant) told us that she once played hostess to an American couple who were visiting the city on business. It is a big deal for the French to invite a foreigner into their home. The French woman, Jeanette, told the Americans that the wine they were drinking was 20 years old. Afterwards she noticed that neither of the Americans had touched the wine; their glasses were still full when they left the table.

'Did you not like the wine?' Jeanette asked, upset.

'We're very particular about sell-by-dates back home,' drawled the American woman. 'If it's 20 years old I'm afraid it must be well past its sell-by-date.'

Fourth, when huge ugly barriers were erected around the American embassy in Paris the story in the city was that the barriers were being put there not to protect the Americans but to keep the Americans shut in to protect the French.

6. The French don't have much of a sense of time

There are very few public clocks in Paris or, indeed, anywhere in France. Spend a few days in Paris and you'll soon see why.

The French seem perfectly capable of going off to lunch at the right time. It's getting back that they find difficult.

7. In France the shop assistant is always right

In many countries shop staff and service employees are taught that the customer is always right. This is not, and never has been, the case in France. In France the employee is always more important than the customer and the customer is always wrong, whatever they might say or do. (The only exceptions are the French themselves. French shoppers dominate a shop in the way that an armoured tank can dominate a village square.)

We do, however, know people who found a way round this. Emigrating friends of ours from East Anglia who had trouble with builders in France hired a friend with a camcorder to follow them around. They told the builder and his team that they were taking part in a British television programme about Britons moving to France. They made sure that word got back to the local mayor too. After that they were very well looked after. 'People couldn't do enough for us,' the former East Anglians told us. 'And the builders finished on time. The best bit was that since the programme was supposedly being made for British television no one complained that they hadn't seen it promoted in the local TV schedules.'

8. The French love dogs

The French are a confusing bundle of contradictions. Nothing illustrates this better than their attitude towards animals. On the one hand the French are the cruellest people on the planet. They hunt and shoot anything that moves and they force feed geese until they nearly burst so that they can make pâté from their livers.

But on the other hand they also love animals and adore them as pets. No one, not even the British, make as much fuss of their pet animals as the French do.

Although most of them live in apartments the Parisians still insist on keeping animals. Because they are French they naturally choose dogs which are in inverse size to the size of their apartments. So, for example, Parisians who live in tiny one roomed studio apartments usually keep Alsatians, Dobermanns or Rottweilers. (The reasoning behind this is typically French. If you are seen out in the park with a huge dog everyone who sees you will assume that you must have an equally huge apartment. It doesn't work, of course, because everyone knows that people with small apartments deliberately choose big dogs for this reason. But French logic doesn't stretch this far.)

Those who can afford larger apartments (such as elderly actresses and call-girls) still favour small dogs which they can carry under their arms and decorate with ribbons and bows to match the day's outfit. One Parisian friend of ours (a woman of indeterminate years but firm opinions who shares her apartment with three cats) insists that any attractive woman who is by herself but accompanied by a small dog must either now be, or must once have been, a prostitute, but we think this may be a potentially dangerous generalisation.

There is a delightful and rather elderly lady who lives in our street. She had a modest career as an actress but a far more successful career as a fiancée. In her twenties she was engaged more often than a public lavatory in central Paris and, as a result of these unsuccessful alliances, put together an impressive collection of jewellery (by no means just rings) which, in her thirties, she sold and converted into property. Today, she is wealthy enough to live in some comfort. She has one of those tiny, hairless dogs which always look as though they are either dying from some terrible disease or have been taking a long course of chemotherapy. Whenever she takes it for a walk she dresses it in something that matches her chosen outfit of the day. For example, yesterday we saw her queuing outside the bread shop. She was dressed in a smart purple jacket while the dog had a matching purple scarf around its neck. She has scarves for the dog which match all her outfits. The inevitable result of all these dogs is that the pavements of Paris are festooned with the inevitable unpleasant consequences. As a result, Parisians develop the 'avoidance side-step' which involves walking around with their eyes fixed firmly on the pavement a yard or two ahead and shuffling and jiggling around the hazards. Visitors who want to avoid taking unpleasant souvenirs back into their hotel rooms are wise to adopt this method of walking, though it does rather spoil one's chances of enjoying the views. A high percentage of elderly Parisians seem to be afflicted with dowager's humps and we suspect that this may be a result of years spent shuffling along the pavements of Paris, ever watchful for the next pile of steaming excrement.

Incidentally, the French don't put up signs saying 'Beware of the dog'. Instead they put up signs saying simply 'Chien méchant'. The words 'chien méchant' do not, of course, mean that there is just a guard dog on the premises. A 'chien méchant' is a wicked dog. We have even seen signs illustrated with slavering dogs which are clearly intended to be rabid.

9. The French love cats too

The French also love cats. It has been reported that one in two Parisians sleeps with a cat every night.

Although Paris is full of cats you won't see many of these animals out and about. The French love their cats so much that they don't usually let them outside where they might get run over. We have, however, seen cats riding both on pedal cycles and motorcycles. The one on a bicycle was sitting in a wickerwork basket attached to the bicycle handlebars. The one riding on a motorbike was sitting in one of the panniers. His head was sticking out of the panier and he was taking a great interest in the world passing by. Neither cat was alone. Both were accompanied by Frenchmen.

In addition to loving cats for all the usual reasons the French have a great deal of respect for cats as hunters. Last year a Scottish friend of ours who was visiting Paris on business spotted a mouse in his hotel room. He rang down and reported this to the reception desk. 'It will be dealt with at once,' he was told. Our Scottish friend repacked his case and waited to be taken to a mouse-free room. He was rather surprised when, a few minutes later, a porter arrived and thrust a cat into his arms. 'The cat will get rid of the mouse for you,' our friend was told.

10. The French love demonstrations

Even if your stay in Paris lasts only for a few days you are quite likely
to see at least one demonstration while you are there. The French
absolutely adore demonstrations. If there isn't at least one major
demonstration ('une manifestation') in Paris each week the papers
start asking questions about the future of democracy.

The demonstrations can be about anything or nothing. Farmers
protest about the meanness of the Common Agricultural Policy (yes,
we know). Hunters protest to confirm their right to shoot anything
that moves (including each other) whenever the shooting takes their
fancy. And, of course, students protest just for the hell of it. We once
saw a demonstration involving lawyers. It was quite surreal to see
hordes of black gowned lawyers marching through the streets with
placards and banners. We can't for the life of us remember what
they were protesting about but it almost certainly doesn't matter
now and it probably didn't matter much then either. Our favourite
demonstration occurred a year or two ago when unemployed French
workers went on strike and blockaded government offices. They
were demanding higher benefit payments and threatening to refuse
to do nothing if they didn't get what they wanted.

Ask a demonstrator what he is demonstrating about and he'll
probably just shrug his shoulders and carry on shouting general
abuse about the Government. Just as there are people in Britain who
routinely attend funerals so, in France, there are people who routinely
attend demonstrations. To the keen funeral goer the identity of the
person in the coffin is of no consequence. To the demonstration
aficionado the subject of the demonstration is irrelevant.

The right to demonstrate or take direct action in France is highly
valued and comes partly from the revolutionary traditions established
in 1789 and partly from the French lack of faith in parliamentary
representation. The French regard their parliament as weak and,
indeed, it is pretty much ignored by the executive and by the French
civil service.

France may be the most bureaucratic country in the world but it
is also a natural home-land for revolutionaries and so politicians take
demonstrations seriously. Street protests have, in the past, toppled
governments and they will doubtless do so in the future.

French demonstrations sometimes look a bit scary but they are usually pretty peaceful and unthreatening affairs and we don't worry too much if we turn a corner and get caught up in one. The lack of aggression is probably a result of the fact that the demonstrators know that they can do pretty much whatever they like (including disrupt the traffic) as long as they finish on time and don't involve the police in any overtime.

The main difference between demonstrations in Britain and France is that while in Britain the police regard all street protestors as potential terrorists, who deserve to have their heads broken and their limbs torn from their bodies, in France the police recognise that demonstrating is a highly responsible, respectable part of everyday social life.

We once watched in amazement as demonstrators lit a huge bonfire in the middle of what was normally a busy Paris street. The demonstrators scavenged bits of wood from building skips and paper from dustbins and lit an impromptu fire that blazed forty or fifty feet into the sky. There wasn't a policeman in sight. Then, as we passed by and approached a nearby corner, we noticed a policeman's head poking around the brickwork. Round the corner, completely out of sight, there were twenty bus loads of policemen and a couple of fire engines. Most of the policemen were sitting playing cards in their buses. They were wearing full body armour but had their helmet visors pushed back so that they could see the cards. (The Parisian police have little tables fixed in the buses so that they can set up little foursomes for cards). The policeman peering round the corner was a lookout keeping an eye on things. Presumably, if the flames had got to some unacceptable height, the watching policeman would have blown his whistle and the card-playing coppers would have dropped their cards and streamed out of their buses to do the necessary.

11. The French don't give a fig about their cars

Millions of British motorists spend their Sunday mornings cleaning and polishing their cars but you would never catch a Frenchman so much as flicking a duster over a motor car. We would hazard a guess that the French market for car polish must be the smallest in the world. The French regard the motor car as a thoroughly overrated piece of equipment. It is neither a status symbol nor a sign of virility.

The British also tend to worry more about minor bumps and scratches than French drivers do. Walk around a major British city and you'll find bumps and dents the exception rather than the rule. Walk around Paris, however, and you'll be hard put to it to find any motor car that hasn't got a few curves that weren't in the original specifications. Most Parisian cars look as if they have spent some time fitted on a pole and being driven round and round a dodgem car enclosure.

On quiet walks along dull avenues you can amuse yourself by counting the number of cars you pass which do have dents or scratches. Our record is 23 damaged cars in a row. You will find that it is difficult to spot more than a tiny proportion of cars which are undamaged. Dents and bumps are so common in French cars that we have a sneaking suspicion that the dealers put them in before they allow their cars onto the road. To be honest we strongly suspect that a good, honest Frenchman (assuming one could be found) would be embarrassed to be seen driving a motor car that didn't have a dent or two in the body work. French motorists certainly don't waste time claiming on their insurance or having their bumps hammered out.

You will probably be spending more of your time in Paris as a pedestrian than as a motorist and so you should be aware that French drivers don't have much of a sense of responsibility as far as pedestrians are concerned.

French drivers tend to park their cars where they happen to stop. Since there are rarely any suitable parking spaces in the city centre this means that they simply park on the first pedestrian crossing they come to, leaving pedestrians with the choice of either squeezing between two sets of bumpers or climbing over the car bonnet. If French drivers want to park on the pavement they regard it as the job of any nearby pedestrian to get out of the way fast.

While on the subject of road safety it is also well worth remembering that traffic lights in Paris are there merely to add a little colour to the motorist's day. Green lights on the roads are a negotiating point but in practice no one stops long enough to do any negotiating. Car, lorry and bus drivers know that they are in an advantaged negotiating position when they are dealing with pedestrians. What sort of damage can even a plump visitor do to a speeding Citroën?

There are speed limits in Paris but it quite clear that most people don't know what they are and the few who do, don't care much about them. If asked to make an informed guess we would say that the usual speed limit within the city is 70 mph. Around the place de la Concorde and the Etoile (at the top of the Champs-Elysées) the speed limit must be somewhere in between 80 mph and 100 mph.

Finally, you should be aware that motorcyclists sometimes ride on the pavement – usually travelling at the sort of speeds you'd expect them to travel on the roads. They, like Sartre and Picasso sitting in a café pretending the Germans aren't even there, are simply doing what the French do best: either ignoring reality, or driving round it.

12. The French are very vain

The French may not care two hoots about what their cars look like but they are very fussy about their personal appearance. The city is crammed with beauty salons and hairdressers. And, in Paris, everyone it seems is an expert on such matters. Even the novelist Colette once opened a chain of beauty salons. (Though, by all accounts, she wasn't terribly good at it. Even her dearest friends said that her clients emerged looking 15 years older.)

A neighbour once told us about a former actress (she was, apparently, something of a star in her now long-forgotten day) who insists on having her hair and make-up done even if she is only having visitors to lunch in her own apartment.

When French singer, songwriter and general superstar Serge Gainsbourg had a heart attack he refused to go to hospital because he didn't like the colour of the blanket the ambulance crew tried to drape over him. The ailing Gainsbourg clambered off the stretcher, crawled into his flat and dragged himself upstairs to find a more acceptable blanket.

13. Elegance and style

The French don't much care what you or they do as long as it is done with style and elegance. When they go camping they take chairs, table, tablecloth, napkins, silverware and a wine cooler. When you buy a single cake in a pâtisserie in Paris the assistant will carefully place your selection on a white cardboard tray, wrap it in pretty paper and then tie the whole thing up with a ribbon so that you can walk out of the shop dangling your purchase from a single finger.

The posh French always set the table with the tines of the fork pointing down against the table cloth rather than up in the air (as most other people usually do). They do this in order to display the family crest on the back of the fork.

Look around in the shops (including the supermarkets) and you will see that Parisian housewives of all ages invariably put on their best frocks to go shopping. They never go out in public without having their hair done and without full make up.

The French continue to care about their appearance however old they get. A twenty-year-old English girl probably doesn't give two hoots about what she will look like in fifty years time. A twenty-year-old French girl does. By the middle of the 21st century British nursing homes are going to be full of elderly women with roses tattooed on their breasts and buttocks. This will not happen in France. French women don't have tattoos; they long ago realised that what might look quite fetching on a 20-year-old girl would look downright silly on a 70-year-old dowager.

Even women in their eighties and nineties totter out with nails, hair and make-up all looking immaculate. In Britain, women of this age would be sitting in red plastic chairs in nursing homes. In Paris, such women have a little apartment (with a budgie or a cat for company) and they do their own shopping and cooking. They never, ever pop out in their curlers and slippers. No one hurries them.

We were in a French department store recently, passing through the bra department, where several acres of expensive lingerie was offered for sale. We saw two women in their seventies who were looking at bras. 'No, this is no good,' said one, discarding a bra she had been looking at. 'This is far too plain. There is not enough lace.'

'Might I be so bold as to ask just who is going to see?' asked the second woman.

'Just me,' replied the first woman rather indignantly. 'That is enough.'

(As an aside it is worth mentioning that the word 'brassière' means a baby's vest in French. The French for what English speakers call a bra is 'soutiens-gorge'. Curiously, the noun is masculine and is, therefore, 'le soutiens-gorge'.)

★ ★ ★

The disappearance of the once famous French pissoirs is a consequence of the French obsession with style and manners over substance. Pissoirs were small, green painted metal facilities which were introduced so that men would no longer have an excuse for urinating in shop doorways. They were extremely popular with cab drivers and bus drivers and they were remarkably simple.

The business part of the erection (the porcelain) was protected from the world by a green metal screen which started about two feet off the ground and finished a few feet higher. There was no roof (so the pissoir was cleaned every time it rained). Passers by could see the feet and heads of those using the pissoir, but they couldn't see the business end of the operation being conducted. One of the last pissoirs to go was the one outside the Ministry of Defence in the rue Saint Dominique.

Pissoirs disappeared after the French Parliament spent days debating whether a gentleman in a pissoir should raise his hat if he recognised a woman passing by. They simply couldn't make up their minds and, in the end, decided that the easiest solution was to get rid of all the pissoirs.

The Government replaced pissoirs with the high tech self-cleaning unisex vacuum modules which we mentioned earlier. These are, no doubt, very sanitary (every few minutes they are hosed down with force and sterilised at a million degrees centigrade, and so if you use one make sure you get out fast afterwards) but they are rather ugly. Photographers used to take wonderfully evocative shots of pissoirs but we can't see anyone bothering to waste pixels on Paris's new modular conveniences.

The French love codes, formalities and style. They love to do things the right way. La règle rules. Everything should be done at the right time and speed, at the right place and in the right way. And while you are doing what you are doing, you must be wearing the right clothes. We suspect that the French would forgive murder if it is was done by someone wearing a well-chosen outfit.

Occasionally, the French obsession with doing things 'comme il faut' (properly) creates problems.

A young French friend of ours called Henri is desperate to look like an Englishman (surprisingly this is a common yearning among French men). He goes about wearing a sports coat, grey flannels and brogues but he doesn't look in the slightest bit like an Englishman.

'Do I look like an Englishman?' Henri asked us. 'You must be honest with me.'

He could tell from our faces that he didn't.

'What is wrong?' he asked.

'None of your jacket buttons are hanging loose from a single thread, your trousers are creased in the right places and the leather patches on your elbows are polished rather than scuffed,' we told him. 'You're trying too hard.'

14. No shame
The French do not understand the meaning of the word embarrassment.

When Helene, the wife of a friend of ours who lives in the 4th arrondissement, told her husband, Jean-Jacques, that she had nothing to wear for an important dinner with a client of his he didn't believe her and wouldn't allow her to buy anything new. This turned out to be a mistake. The two of them have separate dressing rooms and met in the hallway of their apartment only when they were ready to leave.

Jean-Jacques had quite a surprise when Helene took off her coat at the client's home. Underneath it she was wearing nothing but a tasteful selection of expensive Parisian lingerie which, being French, revealed far more than it hid. 'But I told you I had nothing to wear,' she told her husband when he protested.

Jean-Jaques took her to Ungaro's in the avenue Montaigne the very next day and bought her two expensive new gowns.

Jean-Jaques is, incidentally, an extremely successful French novelist. Under several feminine pen names he writes romantic fiction which appeals to women of all ages. Ten years ago he realised that his audience would be more enthusiastic about his books if he could promote them on television. He realised, however, that he couldn't do this because all his pen names were female. (When French women buy romantic fiction they expect it to be written by a woman.) And so he hired a young actress to pretend to be him. Or, rather, to pretend to be the author he was pretending to be. The young actress signed a secrecy agreement and agreed to do promotional appearances on radio and television. She read all his books and rehearsed a series of bright anecdotes with which to entertain listeners and viewers. After six months (and dramatically increased sales figures) the author and the actress fell in love. Despite the incident with the missing dress they are now very happily married. Jean-Jaques and Helene, the two halves of the romantic authoress have been joined together.

15. The elderly in Paris

The elderly in Paris are universally dignified. They go for walks, they play boules, they exercise their dogs, they sit in cafés, they have a drink in a bar. They do not wear hideous elastic waisted trousers, live in ghettos and travel around on coaches.

Traditionally, the French look after their old people. The elderly make good babysitters who are cheap and can, usually, be relied upon not to sleep with monsieur. Sadly, however, the reputation of the French for looking after their elderly took something of a hit recently when, during a heatwave, tens of thousands of elderly Parisians died alone and unnoticed in their boiling hot apartments while their families were away at the beach.

16. The French royal family

Although it is entirely their own fault, the French regret no longer having a royal family.

They do, of course, borrow the British Royal Family when they feel the need. Some French popular magazines still regularly carry stories about Princess Diana.

To replace a hereditary royal family the French have Johnny Hallyday.

Monsieur Hallyday is a singer, actor and personality who became a star in France at about the same time as Elvis Presley became a star in America. He is a big a star in France as Elvis was almost everywhere else. You can get some idea of Johnny's popularity when we tell you that his last double album sold over two million copies on its first day of sale. Go into a record store and you will see almost all his old albums still on sale.

It is rare to visit Paris and not see posters advertising a new Johnny Hallyday album, film, television special, concert, autobiography or magazine feature. The guy seems to have done everything and to be everywhere. Astonishingly, he has even made a cowboy film.

Occasionally, Monsieur Hallyday will perform a free concert to a million or so of his closest admirers. One, which was held underneath the Eiffel Tower, attracted a crowd which stretched all the way back to the École Militaire. Stand underneath the Tower and look away from the river. The adoring crowd lasted as far as you can see and included young couples with babies as well as grandparents.

Monsieur Hallyday is a phenomenon. If he ever puts himself up for election he will doubtless become President.

17. The French police

We sat one day in a café reading about marauding, murdering gangs of feral youths in Britain. We tried to decide when we had last seen policemen in Britain who weren't sitting in a car on a motorway bridge. One of us said we thought we'd seen two policemen in a car the previous April. The other remembered the incident but said that the police were parked in a side road waiting for speeding motorists so that didn't really count. Neither of us could remember seeing a policeman's legs for several years.

In Britain we have grown accustomed to the fact that most of our policemen spend most of their time sitting in comfortable cars or vans on motorway bridges or behind trees, waiting for motorists to whizz past so that they can earn some money for the Government and their local police force.

In Paris, you will actually see policemen wandering around. Spend a day in Paris and by the end of it you will have probably seen policemen patrolling in cars, on motorbikes, on mountain bikes, in vans, on roller blades, on foot and on horseback. Some will have been in twos, some in threes and some in little clusters. Quite a few will have been smiling. The policemen in Paris will actually give advice to tourists who are lost without demanding to see identification or shooting them seven times in the head.

If you get a chance, by the way, do lose something and totter into the local police station to make a report. You will probably find yourself reporting to a detective who has a cigarette hanging from one corner of his mouth. He will wear a trenchcoat with the collar turned up and squint a good deal (possibly as a result of the rising plume cigarette smoke). A third of French policemen look like Jean Gabin, a third look like Jean-Paul Belmondo and the rest look like Alain Delon. The French police pick out their reports on old-fashioned sit up and beg typewriters left over from the black and white movies.

18. The French are quick to learn
You must not give the French ideas

An English banker friend of ours was sitting in the notaire's office, buying an apartment to use as a pied à terre.

'Will you be leaving the fixtures and fittings?' he asked.

The people selling the apartment looked at him with raised eyebrows.

'The light fittings, bathroom cupboards, things like that.'

'Do English people take these?' they asked, unable to disguise their astonishment.

'I'm afraid some do,' he confessed, feeling ashamed of his countrymen; embarrassed that they would do such things.

'Really?' said the French couple. 'They take the bathroom cupboard?' They looked at the notaire. He shrugged.

'A couple I know bought a house,' continued our friend, 'and when they got there even the doors and the skirting boards had gone.'

'No! This cannot be!' said the shocked couple. 'Surely no one would do such a terrible thing.'

'I'm afraid so,' said our friend, now feeling much more comfortable about the flat he was buying. 'Whenever I have bought a house the previous owners have removed everything they could,' he explained. 'They all told the lawyers that they would leave stuff. And then took it. The bathroom cupboard, the light fittings, the curtains, the carpets, the television aerial – all that stuff. Someone I know got to their new home and found that the lawn had been rolled up and taken away.'

'Good heavens,' said the French couple. 'How terrible.' They tutted and shook their heads. 'It is unbelievable,' they said.

'This terrible thing does not happen here,' said the notaire firmly. The French couple both nodded.

When our friend got the key to his new apartment he rushed round, full of excitement at owning a piece of Paris.

Everything that could be moved, unscrewed or prised away from the walls had gone.

19. Non!

An Italian publisher friend of ours (a man who loves Paris but is not quite so sure about the Parisians) insists that the first word of French that a baby learns is 'Non' and that the first complete sentence is 'It is not possible.' He claims, however, that he has found the answer to this negativity. When asking for something to be done he begins with: 'I am sure this is not possible. Am I right?' He then explains what he wants. Being contrary the French will usually insist that they can do the impossible. So, for example, when speaking to a workman our friend might say: 'I know, of course that it would not be possible to do (whatever it is) because there are no workmen around these days who can do those things.' He says that the workmen always become very indignant and say that although for others it may be impossible, they can do it.

20. The French are very formal

If you speak French do not ever make the mistake of referring to a stranger as 'tu'. The French reserve 'tu' for very close family and extremely close friends. They do not 'tutu' strangers.

One of the many men who have repaired our heating system once told us that he knew a married couple in their 70's who, despite having been married for over forty years and having had four children, had still not got to the point where they called one another 'tu'.

Even he thought this rather unusual.

But it happens.

21. The French love music

In our apartment building in Paris there is one saxophonist, one violinist, one pianist and one accordionist. Plus one baby. Sometimes all these musicians choose to play together. They open their windows so that they can share their music with their neighbours. Naturally this wakes up the baby who adds his own particular brand of music to the ensemble. But it's real, it's human and it's lovely.

22. Civic efficiency

Apart from their affection for dogs (and their willingness to allow them to defecate everywhere) the Parisians are very proud of their city's cleanliness. And, to be fair, it is probably the cleanest capital city in the world. The streets are swept constantly, water is flushed along the gutters every day (via a magnificent system which relies on bits of old sacking tied together with string to direct the water in the approved direction) and rubbish is collected daily. We heard banging at 9 p.m. one Saturday evening. We looked out of the window and saw the dustmen emptying the bins (they were a bit late that night but they still came).

As more and more of Britain moves to a rubbish collection once a fortnight Paris's still daily collections are a sign of a civilisation refusing to fail.

23. The arty farty French

The French are very arty and the Parisians are more arty than anyone anywhere else in France.

If your French is good enough you could try going to the theatre. There are many theatres in Paris and at least one will always be doing something by Molière (who is to the French what Shakespeare is to everyone else but who is, we hate to have to admit it, sometimes wittier and sharper). Molière was the world's first real social satirist.

Other than works by Molière there are two plays performed at French theatres. In the first play two men dress up as women. There is always a good reason for this of course. In the second play a middle aged man has a young mistress. They are getting to know one another in the family bed when the man's wife comes home and catches them. There is then much rushing about and a great deal of opening and shutting of doors.

If you prefer cinema to theatre you will be thoroughly spoilt for choice, though be warned: French cinema goers like to make cinema more exciting by missing the first 5 minutes, making a noticeable entrance and then having to spend the next 90 minutes (or whatever) trying to work out what is happening by whispering loudly to one another.

If you want to see a film in the original language (e.g. English) simply look out for a film being shown in the 'version originale' (you will see the letters V.O. somewhere on the poster or above the ticket queue).

Working out the titles isn't always easy, however. You might imagine that film titles would be translated in a fairly straightforward manner with the result that well known films might become: *Les Frères Bleux (The Blues Brothers)*, *Le Son de Musique (The Sound Of Music)*, *Disparu avec le Vente (Gone With The Wind)*, *Quel q'un l'Aime Chaud (Some Like It Hot)* and *Pour Quelques Dollars Encore (For A Few Dollars More)*.

But this is France and things aren't done in such an obvious way. In an attempt to put their own stamp onto a film the French will usually give it a title which bears no resemblance to a translation of the original. So, for example, *Les Frères Bleux* would probably be advertised as *Les Soeurs du Nuit*. Go figure if you have the time. Alternatively, you can probably guess what is showing by looking at the posters and reading the small print.

24. Essential advice if you need to abuse a Frenchman

If you spend time in Paris then, sooner or later, you will need to abuse a Frenchman (or woman). This is just the way things are and it is no shame on you or the French person you will be abusing.

When this happens there is one very important thing to remember: however well you speak French you should revert to English.

English friends of ours who are quite fluent in French admit that they always revert to English when they need to berate a workman, traffic warden or difficult concierge.

'I always freeze and forget what I want to say if I try to shout in French,' admits the husband, who, to our ear, speaks French like a native. 'You are at a huge disadvantage if you try to have a row in their language,' he says. 'Their invective will always be better than yours. Your only chance of getting the upper hand is to shout in English. You will know better words and whereas you might recognise something of what they are saying there is a chance that, if you show sufficient imagination, they won't have the faintest idea what you are saying. If you should lose your temper and say something quite unforgivable there is a chance that you will get away with it because they won't know what you've said.'

25. Speaking French (or not)

Apart from the English and the Americans, the French are the only people in the world who expect strangers to speak their language.

What will de Gaulle find to talk about to God, Noel Coward was once asked. 'It depends,' murmured Coward, 'on how good God's French is.'

But whereas the British and the Americans always try to help foreigners who don't speak English by raising their voices and shouting a good deal the French tend to just tut and smile and to shake their heads in that infuriating Gallic way that tells you that although they aren't saying anything downright rude they think that you're really, really stupid and inferior to them and that this is entirely due to the fact that you had the misfortune to be born foreign and not French. It's not your fault, of course, so they don't blame you. They just feel sorry for you.

The French like foreigners (that's us) to try and speak their language because it enables them to correct our grammar or our pronunciation or, preferably, both. This makes them feel superior and, therefore, very pleased with themselves. The French, more than any other nation on earth, like feeling pleased with themselves. If there is one word which sums up the French it is 'smug'. They are often quite jolly people. But they are always smug.

It is crucial to remember that if you try to speak French then however you choose to say it, and whatever you choose to say, something you say will be wrong. You must not take offence at this. It is just the way the French like to put you down and show that they are superior to you.

When a friend of ours called Kenneth first visited Paris he ordered a Pernod in a famous pavement café which we won't mention because it's the Café de la Paix in the place de l'Opera and we want to be able to go back there. The waiter stared at him, clearly puzzled. 'Purnow?' he said, wrinkling up his nose and shaking his head. Kenneth pointed to the menu to explain what he wanted. 'Ah!' said the waiter, understanding. 'Pairnew.' Our friend nodded, grateful for the correction.

The next time Kenneth went into the same café (which we still won't name because it's still the Café de la Paix) he ordered a 'Pairnew.' The waiter stared at him as if he'd asked for a plate of fish and chips with lots of salt and vinegar and extra batter bits. Once again Kenneth had to go through the ritual of pointing to the relevant line in the menu. 'Ah!' said the waiter. 'Purnow!'

Kenneth left Paris convinced that café waiters go to special classes where they practise tricks designed to make their customers look like idiots. He was mistaken. There are no special classes. French waiters do this quite instinctively.

There's an old joke about an Englishman in Paris who called over the waiter.

'Waiter, there is a fly in my soup,' said the Englishman. The waiter stared at him, uncomprehendingly.

'Un mouche,' said the Englishman, pointing to the soup and the offending insect.

The waiter peered at the fly. 'Ah, non, monsieur c'est une mouche,' said the waiter. 'The fly is feminine.'

The Englishman looked down. 'How the hell can you see that?' he demanded.

Of course, you don't really need to speak French at all in Paris.

Most French people (and all French people in Paris) speak English when they want you to do something for them (such as give them money) although they don't speak a word of it when you want them to do something for you.

Most French people (and nearly all the ones you are likely to meet as a traveller in Paris) speak perfectly passable English (though their grammar and punctuation sometimes need correcting and, generally speaking, we hope you will do this for them).

Remember this at all times: however much they pretend they don't understand or speak English they do.

English is very much the language of Europe these days. It is the language of the Internet, the language of medicine and science and the language of money. The French don't like this, of course, but that's just their hard luck. Club de golf is the official Academie Française French for golf club. That says it all, really, doesn't it?

If you have something difficult to do simply insist that the conversation is conducted in English. This will put the French in a position of inferiority and it will put you in charge of the conversation.

These days, we don't much care so much about the French being so snooty about their language because when they speak English they invariably make an enormous mess of things. They all think that they speak perfect English and are far too arrogant to realise what enormous clangers they have made.

Sometimes, just for fun, we don't tell them what fools they are making of themselves and, on occasion, as a special treat, nor should you.

One French acquaintance of ours, who is proud of his wife's cooking, tells everyone he meets who speaks English: 'My wife has made herself into a wonderful tart and everyone who has ever had a taste agrees with me.' We always nod wisely and let him carry on sharing this delightful piece of news with others whom he wishes to impress.

'Slimmers are just fat losers,' the same acquaintance once said when translating and explaining the word 'slimmer' for his wife. She went to a dinner with some Americans in Neuilly and had to run for her life when she repeated his definition. We felt guilty for several microseconds when we heard this. But it's difficult to feel truly guilty when you are convulsed with laughter.

26. The well-mannered French

The French are gloriously unpredictable and inconsistent; sometimes they are extremely polite, sometimes they are very rude and sometimes they are both at once. On occasion, the French can be the rudest people in the world. (They've had a lot of practice at it.) Paradoxically, they are sometimes the most well-mannered.

When we finish a letter in English we sign off with 'Yours sincerely'. When the French finish a letter they sign off with: 'Nous vous prions d'agréer monsieur, l'assurance de nos sentiments respecteux' (which roughly translates as we beg you to believe, sir, in the assurance of our respectful sentiments).

If you buy something in a Parisian shop and say 'thank you' to the assistant, he or she will automatically snap back insistently with: 'Non, c'est moi qui vous remercie'. (No, it's me who thanks you).

Even the children are relatively well behaved in France. Walk around Paris and you will see school children going to or from the park in neat rows of two. Each pair of children will be well-dressed and holding hands. This is something we don't see in Britain these days; largely because even six-year-olds have a syringe in one hand and a knife in the other and so cannot possibly hold hands with one another.

27. The French don't 'get' irony

Near to the Eiffel Tower we saw a poster attached to the glass door of a small shop. The words on the poster were: 'Vivre ensemble, pas sans vous' and there was a picture of a man in a wheelchair facing a row of steps. The message was simple: we must all live together. The disabled must not be excluded.

The irony, apparently unnoticed by the shopkeeper who had put the poster in his window, was that in order to enter that particular shop customers had to climb up a massive step. No wheelchair could have ever possibly been manoeuvred into that emporium.

Wonderful.

28. The French and their health

The French drink and smoke to excess but they care passionately about the food they choose to eat. Mortality rates show that although the French have the highest incidence of liver disease in the known world they have a relatively low incidence of heart disease.

Watch Parisian workmen buying their luncheon and you'll see what we mean. Local workmen often buy their lunch in one or other of the supermarkets near where we live. They will buy themselves a freshly baked baguette, a piece of brie or camembert or a slice of ham. They will pick out a fresh apple for desert. They will wash this down with a bottle of water or a bottle of wine. In nutritional terms that's a far cry from the British workman's lunch of a burger or a pie and chips and a pint of beer .

It's not surprising that the French have less heart trouble.

(It would, incidentally, be a mistake to assume that the French prefer simple foods because they cannot be bothered with more complicated arrangements. When workmen were painting our building they drank filtered coffee at break time. We know this because we saw the used filters and coffee grounds in the rubbish they had discarded.)

The French, a nation of hypochondriacs if ever there was one, are obsessed with their health and have four main eccentricities relating to their health.

First, they believe that all health problems are caused by liver troubles. And, considering the amount of wine they drink they are probably right. They believe that everything that goes wrong with them is caused by a faulty liver. It is because of this that they consume so much mineral water. Go into a supermarket and you'll see dozens of different varieties of water on the shelves. They supplement the mineral water with all sorts of weird and wonderful potions. There are as many pharmacies as bakeries in our arrondissement. That's a lot of pharmacies.

Second, they do a great deal of self-diagnosing. They don't use general practitioners in the way that the British do. If they feel ill they decide what is wrong with them and take themselves off to a specialist. It's the French patient, not a general practitioner, who decides what sort of -ologist is required.

Third, the French prefer suppositories to tablets. This is actually quite wise since suppositories are usually less likely to produce unpleasant or dangerous side effects.

Fourth, the French always do what their doctors tell them to do. (French doctors who want to keep their patients never tell them to stop drinking alcohol.) One of our neighbours told us a story about her sister which illustrates this blind obedience very well. The woman was diagnosed as suffering from a fatal disease and was told by the doctor to put her affairs in order. Puzzled but compliant the woman went home and made a list (date, places and names) of all the affairs she had had. (She presumably thought it was some sort of catharsis, designed to make her passing easier.) She then put the fatal list in a drawer in the family bureau and forgot all about it. Three weeks later the woman's doctor told her that a terrible (but at the same time wonderful) mistake had been made by the laboratory. She didn't have a fatal disease and wasn't going to die after all. The woman was overwhelmed with joy. She and her husband celebrated for a week. They had dinner at expensive restaurants. They went to the theatre. And they decided to give up work and to move to the country. It was during the preparations for the move that the husband found the list the woman had made of all her lovers.

The story does, however, have a happy ending. Far from being angry, the husband was very understanding. He said he hadn't realised that his wife had so many 'friends' in Paris and would she really prefer to stay in the city? The woman thought about it for a day or two and finally admitted that, given the choice, she thought she'd settle for retiring and staying in Paris.

So, that's what they did.

We suspect that if the husband ever put his affairs in order his list would be even longer than his wife's.

29. The French are only interested in the best

If you walk around Paris for a while you will notice that while one bread shop in a neighbourhood has an enormous queue outside it the bread shop just a hundred yards down the road will be deserted. In Britain the people in the long queue would simply go to the other shop. In France they don't.

The reason for this is simple.

The bread shop with the queue is the one where the baker is constantly making fresh bread. And he is making good bread. Everyone walks out with something warm in their hand. None of them are carrying a pre-wrapped sliced loaf.

There are, of course, dozens of different types of bread available in his shop (and many different types and sizes of baguette). He uses the best ingredients and makes the best bread in the arrondissement.

The shop down the road has no customers because the baker only bakes two or three times a day, or maybe just every four hours or so. He cannot afford to keep baking bread because he has no customers. It is the baker's Catch 22. How can he possibly obtain a queue of his own without making lorry loads of unsold bread?

(A baker which sold bread baked the day before would last about as long in France as a pub which sold only lemonade would last in Britain.)

30. French slimmers

A man who helped paint our apartment told us that his wife, whom he described as 'plump', was a member of a slimming club in the 18th arrondissement, where they live. She and her fellow slimmers had weekly meetings in a local café which had a tremendous reputation for serving excellent but inexpensive meals. They drank a glass of mineral water each and they weighed themselves on a pair of scales which belonged to the café owner. At the end of each weekly meeting the women had a seven course meal. (The attendees were all women. No Frenchman would ever attend a slimming club.) The painter told us that his wife and her friends never lost any weight but had a great time together on their night out. He said he suspected that none of them really wanted to lose weight because, if they did, they'd have to give up their weekly meetings. The painter told us that his wife had been a member of the club for nearly a year and that during the year she had gone up two dress sizes but claimed to have lost 5kg in weight.

He told us that he thought the café owner was manipulating the scales so that although the women were, in reality, getting heavier they constantly thought that they were getting lighter.

It's the sort of thing the French would do. It enables them to feel good about themselves without ever having to face the unpleasantness of reality.

31. Kissing and shaking
The French do a lot of kissing. An English friend of ours called Richard works as an editor in a publishing office with nine other people – all French. Each morning all the employees have to kiss one another. 'It is nearly time to go for lunch by the time we get through this complicated but essential ritual,' says Richard. 'After the kissing is done all the women have to go off to repair their lipstick. There is no air kissing (known as mwah mwah kissing) in France. These are proper kisses.'

Kissing is now a global phenomenon. In America, women greeting one another confine themselves to one kiss (kisses are usually on the lips rather than on the cheek or in the air). In Austria, Britain, Hungary, Spain and Sweden two kisses are considered de rigeur. Egypt, Russia, Belgium, Holland and Switzerland are three kiss countries.

But it all started in France.

Standard French kissing (as practised in the French provinces and now one of France's most popular exports) has for years involved three moves: a kiss on the left cheek, a kiss on the right cheek and finally a kiss on the left cheek again. The de luxe French kiss, as practised in Paris, adds a final right cheek kiss to this barrage of osculatory activity.

In addition to kissing one another a great deal the French love shaking hands. Another friend of ours, a young Dutchman who works in a rather formal Parisian bank, tells us that shaking hands takes up an hour every morning. As they arrive at the bank each person must shake hands with everyone else. Since there are 17 people in the office where he works this means that each person must shake hands with 16 other people. 'One or two also kiss each other,' says our Dutch friend. 'They usually do the kissing after the formal shaking.'

When we visit our usual supermarket in Paris the manager comes over to greet us and shake hands. (We confess that we quite like this. It makes us feel wanted.)

The French even shake hands when they are in informal situations. We once sat on a beach in the South of France and watched in amazement as two groups of semi-naked people spent ten minutes shaking hands with one another.

32. The best French law

In France it is against the law to ignore someone needing help. Failure to offer assistance to a person in distress is a criminal offence under paragraph 2 of article 63 of the French penal code. This applies to everyone and is, in our view, the best piece of French legislation in existence.

33. Staying cool

There is a card headed 'what-to-do-in-an-emergency' in the hallway of an apartment building near to ours. Printed on the card, in large letters, are the words: 'Gardez Votre Sang-Froid'. 'Keep Your Self Control'. Just that. Nothing else. The French don't like to be seen to panic. It simply isn't cool.

34. Waving not drowning

The French wave their hands and arms around a good deal when they are talking. Naturally, they still do this when they are using their hands-free mobile telephones. When we first saw this happening we were rather startled. We were walking along the avenue Montaigne when we spotted a guard in a uniform standing outside an upmarket jewellery store. He was waving both arms in the air as though fighting off a swarm of bees. When we got closer we could hear him talking. But there was no one within yards of him. Only on fairly close examination did we spot the tiny earpiece and the microphone pinned on his tie. What made the incident particularly unnerving was that before we saw the earpiece and the microphone we noticed that he was wearing a gun in a holster around his waist.

On another occasion we watched in astonishment as two Frenchmen sat opposite one another at a table in La Rhumerie café in St Germain des Prés. (It's one of our favourite cafés. They serve the best grog in Paris.) The two men were both shouting and waving their arms about. It was only when one of the men got up and left, and the other continued to rave and wave, that we realised that the two men didn't know one another. They were both talking on their mobile telephones and were sharing a table simply because the café was crowded.

35. Open spaces

The French live in a country with a lot of open spaces and are not accustomed to being too crowded. They enjoy the feeling of having some space around them. There are five times as many cars per mile of British road as there are per mile of French road and there are four times as many people per square mile in Britain as there are in France. The French are accustomed to large open spaces and empty roads rather than huge urban sprawls and over-crowded motorways.

It is because of this affection with the countryside that modern France is run for the farmers. Most French farmers (and there are millions of them) tend to have one small field each. In their field they either grow turnips or keep a sheep. They live on huge grants from the European Union (EU). The Common Agricultural Policy (which ensures the survival of these tiny farms) is not a consequence of the EU it is the reason for its existence.

(The French love the bureaucracy created by the EU – most of it of French origin – because they ignore the rules they don't like. They know that the British and the Germans will stick to the letter of every law and thereby slowly ruin themselves.)

The Parisians would never dream of spending more than two weeks among green pastures but they like to think of themselves as country folk.

36. Boules

The French love playing their version of bowls (which they call boules). Walk through a park of any size and you will probably see a group of people playing boules. Summer or winter, wet or dry they will be there. Most players are men aged between 30 and 100. Each man has two boules and, as in the English game, the aim is to get your balls closest to the jack. But since they play on fairly rough ground they throw, rather than bowl, their balls.

It's a truly relaxing game to play or watch. It involves virtually no physical exercise at all (players even use magnets on lengths of string so that they can pick up their boules without having to bend down) and absolutely no stress. We have watched hundreds of boules matches and never once seen a player become agitated or distressed. Equipment is painfully simple and cheap to purchase. Games are, for the most part played in silence. At the end of a game everyone shakes hands with everyone else and then goes home. Matches are usually informal and of no consequence to anyone, least of all the players.

Although most of the players are men, we do know of one woman who plays regularly. When her husband died the bunch of men he played with asked her if she would like to take his place. So she took over his boules, his boules bag, his magnet and his piece of string. Now she plays boules every afternoon between 2 p.m. and 4 p.m. except when the Tour de France is in progress.

Incidentally, there are two versions of boules. The original variety of the game allows players to take a run up of one or two paces before letting go of the boule. This is known as the 'jeu provençale' version. The rules were changed in Marseilles to accommodate a player called Jules Le Noir who was confined to a wheelchair as a result of an accident. So that he could carry on playing boules the other players voted to change the rules so that players had to stand (or sit) in a rough circle scratched in the dirt. Run ups were banned. The locals described it as playing 'pieds tanques' (feet together) and so petanque was born. Today there are over 50 countries in the International Federation of Petanque.

37. French chefs
Chefs in Britain tend to become famous as a result of their (usually bad) behaviour or their eccentricities. In France, chefs acquire reputations because of the food they produce.

We heard recently about a Parisian chef who had succeeded in turning a single egg white into a cubic metre of meringue. To us this seemed a nonsense; a sort of reverse of the biblical feeding of the five thousand. The chef had taken a perfectly good piece of food and turned into a confection which would feed no one. But to the French this was food as art.

In another fashionable restaurant a Parisian chef made a name for himself by serving a whole meal on five spoons, carefully arranged on the plate. The waitress told diners in which order they should drain their spoons. That was it. Diners didn't even get a slice from a baguette.

A chef who specialises in making hand-made ice cream (he calls himself a glacier) refuses to sell his fine produce when the weather is hot because he fears that people will buy it and eat it to keep cool rather than for the taste.

Only in Paris could this happen.

38. Long lunches
The French believe in lengthy lunches. They like to give themselves time to enjoy their food and they like to give their stomachs time to digest what they have eaten. One of our local supermarkets shuts for two hours at lunchtime every day. No one in Paris raises an

eyebrow. Meals – and meal times – are taken very, very seriously. The French take two hours for lunch because that is the length of time it takes a horse to have a proper feed.

In Britain the British eat because they will die if they don't. The French, in contrast, live to eat. The British take little or no pleasure from the food they consume. The French extract every possible pleasure from eating.

One Englishman we know, waiting for a village shop to open, noticed an old man sitting on a bench lunching off a baguette and a bottle of wine. He wandered over and asked the old man if he knew when the shop opened.

'Half past two,' replied the old man.

The Englishman sat down beside him.

The old man ate his lunch, slowly, and then sat and basked in the sun for another half an hour.

The Englishman, growing impatient, stood up and walked over to the shop. He peered in through the door and then walked up and down.

At two thirty precisely the old man stood up, packed up the remains of his picnic and then wandered over to the shop. And opened it.

Quite right too.

Doubtless such a man is forever a stranger to indigestion.

39. The French as bureaucrats

The French are the most enthusiastically bureaucratic nation on earth. They regard bureaucracy as just as essential to life as wine or good bread. However unlike the Germans (who take their bureaucracy very seriously and regard it as the framework upon which society is built) the French only like bureaucracy because without it they would have nothing to ignore or to rebel against. The English grumble about bureaucrats but do as they are told. The Germans adore bureaucracy. They do as they are told the minute they are told to do it. The French do what they are told to do. But they do it when they want to do it.

If they are troubled by bureaucrats the French send back long, complicated letters which require a good deal of consideration before they can be answered. Relatively simple disputes between citizens and bureaucrats can go on for generations.

Nevertheless, the joke is really on the French because the cost of all the bureaucracy in France is destroying the country. The French economy is burdened by the cost of state owned industries, by too much bureaucracy (with excessively generous pension schemes for State employees) and by a welfare and benefit system which, like Britain's, is far too expensive.

An even higher proportion of French employees work for the State than is the case in Britain. In France something like one in three people who receive a pay packet receive their monthly cheque from the Government. It isn't difficult to find examples of over-manning. The railways, for example, are notoriously overstaffed. Everyone in France wants to work for the French railways (cynics say that most people do) because railway workers, known as 'cheminots', have for years been able to retire at the age of 50 on full pay. The massive pension fund which pays for this wonderfully over-generous gesture is, of course, largely provided by taxpayers.

On a train from Paris to Vernon (a small town just a few miles outside the capital) our tickets were examined by no less than eleven inspectors.

Overmanning isn't confined to the railways, of course. We once sat in a café in Paris and watched five men change the printed time table in a small display box at a bus stop. The five men were accompanied by a supervisor in a grey suit who made sure that each man carried out his official activity. It was funnier than watching a BBC television crew in the 1980's.

Bureaucracy has now entered all aspects of French life. The last time we bought furniture in the huge, old store called La Samaritaine (at the northern end of the Pont Neuf) it took us three minutes to choose a desk and three hours to complete the paperwork.

But although the French love making rules they are very, very good at finding ways round them when they want to. Most of the red tape which is now destroying the British economy comes from Brussels and was inspired by the French. But the worst of the red tape is ignored in France. If the French find something inconvenient they will quickly find a way of avoiding it.

For example, an English acquaintance of ours who wanted to retire to France bought a plot of land in a small village, and obtained planning permission to build a small house on it. She then had to go back to Britain (where she worked as a supply teacher) so that she could save up enough money to buy the necessary materials and to pay the builders. When she returned to France she realised to her horror that her planning permission had expired before she had started to build her dream house. In desperation she went to the local Town Hall and spoke to someone in the mayor's office. The bureaucrat listened patiently and sympathetically but the news he gave her was bad. 'If your builders have not started the work then you will have lost your permission,' said the bureaucrat. 'You must re-apply.' He paused and shrugged and sighed. 'Sadly, there are now new rules to take into consideration and it is likely that you will not receive your permission this time.' Our acquaintance burst into tears when she heard this. She had invested everything she had in this project. It was her dream. 'Have you bought any tools?' asked the bureaucrat, softening. 'Just a spade,' replied the teacher, who had purchased the spade so that she could plant a small bush she had been given by a friendly neighbour. 'Ah, then all is well,' said the bureaucrat smiling. 'You have bought a spade and so you have started your building. Your planning permission is intact.'

Part 4: The Twenty Villages of Paris

Introduction

Although the city has a mayor, a town hall (mairie) and all the associated trimmings, Paris is sub-divided into twenty arrondissements. There are no physical barriers, or even any signs telling you when you are leaving one arrondissement and entering another, but the boundaries are there nevertheless – and are extremely important to the Parisians themselves. Each arrondissement has its own mayor and town hall and all the associated trimmings. The arrondissements are self-contained villages, each with its own character, each with its own proud and faithful residents (believing that their arrondissement has unique qualities which make it the very best in the city), its own shops and its own artisans. The people of Paris tend to be as proud of the arrondissement in which they live as they are of the city itself, and local politicians fight hard to protect the history, dignity, efficiency and quality of life in their own small part of Paris. When the end of year report is published each local mayor takes great pride in having provided the residents of his or her arrondissement with better kept parks, more effective traffic control, better street cleaning, better rubbish collecting and more cultural amenities than their neighbours.

The way the city is broken up and organised works well and all the arrondissements really do have their own character and special qualities. All, too, have local shops and services ensuring that, in theory at least, it is perfectly possible for residents to live comfortably within their arrondissement, without having to venture into neighbouring territory.

So seriously is all this regarded that individuals, shops and offices in the big telephone directory for Paris are listed according to the arrondissement in which they can be found.

(Incidentally, just to confuse visitors, the French will sometimes talk about the quartier or the neighbourhood in which they live. Depending upon the speaker they may be referring to their arrondissement, a part of an arrondissement or a piece of the city which crosses over two different arrondissements. Ignore all such talk and concentrate on arrondissements.)

The arrondissements are arranged in a spiral starting from the centre of Paris, an arrangement sometimes described as being designed rather like a snail's shell (comme un escargot) which, given the unique French affection for dealing with their garden pests by the simple expedient of eating them, seems appropriate.

The first eight arrondissements are in the very centre of Paris and the other twelve, which tend to be larger, run around the outside. The first arrondissement is right in the middle of the city and just north of the River Seine. The other 19 arrondissements are numbered clockwise from the first.

We have prepared a thumbnail sketch for each of the 20 arrondissements of Paris – drawing attention to what we think are the very best bits of each.

1st Arrondissement

Of all the arrondissements the 1st is the one most dedicated to tourism. The arrondissement covers a small area of the city but includes the Palais du Louvre (the former royal palace which has been home to France's most famous museum since 1791), the Jardin des Tuileries, the Musée de l'Orangerie (wherein you will find a magnificent collection of impressionist paintings – including Claude Monet's finest water lilies) – the place Vendome, a big chunk of the rue de Rivoli, the most important part of the rue Saint Honoré and a lot of very high class (and rather dull) hotels where most of the guests in residence are people who aren't paying their own bills.

If you go anywhere near the Louvre museum do go and see the glass pyramid in the courtyard. The pyramid, designed by I.M.Pei and approved by President Mitterand, is the new entrance to the museum and it is very beautiful (particularly at night). The Mona Lisa and the Venus de Milo are both in the Denon wing of the Louvre. You can find them either by following the signposts or by following the crowds. The Venus de Milo was almost destroyed by fire in the 19th century. She was saved when a radiator burst and put her out.

You won't find many signs of 'normal' Paris in the 1st. The shops (and there are a lot of them in the 1st) tend to cater to tourists rather than locals. You're more likely to find shops selling postcards and little models of the Eiffel Tower, rather than shops selling cauliflowers or boxes of camembert. Upmarket stores devote themselves to finding ways to convince overweight American matrons that a crocodile handbag is a snip at 10,000 euros.

There is a wonderful boating pond in the Jardin des Tuileries. You can rent a toy sailboat, and a stick to catch it with, or just sit (no charge) and watch others play with the boat and stick they've rented. A fountain in the middle of the pool keeps the water (and the boats) moving. It's almost too romantic to be true.

For much of the summer you will also find an excellent and colourful traditional fair in the Jardin des Tuileries. There are no hooligans but lots of fun, traditional rides (including some classic beauties) and the inevitable candyfloss stalls. There's also a climbing wall. (Rock climbing is enormously popular in France – probably because the country has more than its fair share of mountains.)

The 1st arrondissement also contains the Jardin du Palais Royale. Nowhere in Paris is quite like the Palais Royale and yet most tourists miss it completely. A few yards off the beaten track and reeking of history the Palais Royale is beautiful, hidden away and very popular as a picnic spot among the Parisians who work in the nearby financial district. Colette lived here and the playwright Molière died in the 'Petit Cardinal' theatre while playing Argan in his own play 'Malade

Imaginaire'. An irony I like to think he would have enjoyed if he hadn't been dead. The Jardin du Palais Royale now contains some rather curious modern art but the whole place is steeped in history and there are still some fascinating shops to be found there underneath the arches. It was here that Paris acquired its first modern café back in the 17th century. Customers at Francesco Procopio dei Costelli's establishment could purchase coffee, hot chocolate, cream of orange flower, oil of Venus (a blend of cinnamon, water, carnation, vanilla and sugar), orange peel liqueur and hippocras (sweet wine spiced with cinnamon, ginger, cloves and mace – a precursor of today's vin chaud).

Paris, incidentally, is packed with parks. Every arrondissement has its fair share of green spaces. Most contain a patch of grass, a few elderly statues (well decorated by Parisian pigeons), a sculpture or two, colourful flower beds, shade-giving plane or horse chestnut trees, a special children's park (admission only to children and adults accompanying them) and plenty of benches.

Parisian parks tend to be formal and well-kept but nonetheless enormously friendly. The French love picnicking and on decent days the best benches in most parks are snapped up early by Parisians unpacking their sandwiches.

We've had some strange experiences having picnics. Sitting in one park in the 1st (not the Palais Royale) a complete stranger came up to us and said: 'You are literary people. You write books.' He then quoted Nietzsche a good deal and took great delight in telling us: 'si vous coupez les tulipes toujours vous avez le potage'. (If you cut the tulips you will always have soup.) We obviously nodded and agreed with him and we trust that if you meet him that you will do the same.

Having le picnic really is one of the best ways to eat in Paris. Wherever you are you won't be far away from a suitable park or square and you will find plenty of comfortable benches to sit on. (Avoid the two sided benches. They're too upright for comfort.) There are so many small shops around that it is never difficult to find the makings for an enjoyable outdoor meal.

Technically, by the way, feeding the birds in Paris is not allowed (though at least they don't seem as keen to lock you up for it as they do in London). However, no one has yet told the birds about the ban on snacking and so they tend to gather if you're having a picnic. If anyone says anything to us about feeding the birds (and occasionally they do, for the French are not slow to remonstrate with strangers) we just apologise and say that we are messy eaters and that the birds are tidying up for us. We once tried this explanation with a policeman. He clearly didn't believe a word of our excuse but he was so pleased with the ingenuity of the explanation that he smiled, peered closely at the variety of cheese we had chosen, nodded approvingly, touched his cap and left us alone.

Apart from the Palais Royale, one of the best picnic spots in the 1st (and, indeed, in the whole of Paris) is the tiny island at the western, pointed end of the Ile de la Cite. About half way across the Pont Neuf you'll find some steps and a notice advertising the boats (Bateaux-Mouches) which fly up and down the river.

Go down the steps and you'll find yourself in a private world known to remarkably few. It's shaped like a triangle so, this being France, it's called the Square du Vert Galant. The flower beds are beautiful and in the early autumn the ground is carpeted with conkers from the horse chestnut trees. To the south of the island, the river fire brigade (the Bateaux Pompes) have their base, just below the quai de Conti on the left bank. If you're lucky they will entertain you while you have your picnic.

We once sat in this small park and watched as an elderly woman and her middle aged son sat down together. They had an old-fashioned leather shopping bag with them. When they were settled and comfortable they opened the bag and took out a pigeon. A live pigeon. The pigeon had a long piece of string tied to its leg. The son tied the other end of the string to the bench and let the pigeon walk about and even fly a little. After an hour or so the couple hauled the pigeon back, untied the string from the bench and returned the bird to the bag. They fastened the top of the bag with two safety pins, then got up and left. We were so intrigued that we went back to the same park the next day. The couple turned up at exactly the same time and did exactly the same thing. No one else seemed to notice.

No one ever notices anything in Paris. Everyone is far too polite and worldly to be surprised or shocked or startled by truly curious behaviour. At the time we contemplated rushing over, cutting the string from the pigeon's foot and letting it go. But (and we're still not quite sure why) we didn't. The strange thing was that the pigeon seemed almost as devoted to the couple as they clearly were to the pigeon. Love and devotion take many different forms.

The Île de la Cité is where Paris began. Part of the original fortress, built by French mediaeval kings, still remains as St Chapelle, a remarkable building which has been standing for 800 years but has still to show its first crack. (Modern builders might like to take a look and check out how it was done.)

Most tourists never walk along the banks of the river Seine, though it's a popular pastime with the Parisians, particularly on a Sunday. The north bank of the river is by far the best, with the stretch between the Pont des Arts and the Pont de la Concorde (in the 1st) being the best stretch. Go down the steps and walk along the bank. Take a book with you and sit on a bench and watch the river and the ducks go by. As you wander you will see barges chugging slowly up the river. The bargemen live on board with their families. They may have their washing hung out to dry and the family car parked bizarrely on the stern. It's difficult not to envy them their small, safe, private worlds; of the world and yet not quite in it, in it and yet not quite of it.

At road level, fixed to the walls which separate the quays from the river, you'll see les bouquinistes – the booksellers whose tiny green boxes or stalls are opened when they feel like it and padlocked when they don't. There you can find books, magazines, posters, and postcards. Most of the items on sale are old, though some are fake. How the stall holders make a living we cannot imagine (though we have a secret theory, previously shared with no one else, that the stalls are mostly run by senior members of the French Government, celebrated authors and Chairmen of large companies, who relax by playing at booksellers in the same way that Marie Antoinette relaxed by playing at being a milkmaid). Walk along one of the quays above the river in September and you will find yourself shuffling through the fruits of the horse chestnut trees. Small French boys don't play conkers and so the fruits lie unwanted and ungathered in the dust. If you have a young relative or friend at home you can quickly fill a bag with conkers while walking along here. (Transporting conkers across the Channel is doubtless illegal so we know you won't do it.) You'll also find plenty of conker trees while walking up the lower reaches of the Champs-Elysées, from the place de la Concorde to le Rond Point.

If you have a suitably equipped penknife with you (and you will need one for picnics – for cutting up baguettes and slicing cheese) bore holes in a couple of horse chestnuts, remove your shoe laces and astonish the locals by playing conkers in the street. They will think you quite eccentric and admire you enormously for it. The French, more than any other nation on earth (more even than the English who more or less invented it) love eccentricity.

The river is, of course, crossed by many bridges. Bridges provide shelter. Tramps need shelter. And so Paris has (and always has had) many tramps living underneath its bridges. The tramps (clochards) are as much a part of the city as are the chestnut trees and the pigeons and although there are occasional protests about them from nouveau riche newcomers, who feel they are an eyesore and should be hidden away somewhere out of sight, the Parisian tramps are largely left alone by the city.

Just how the tramps got where they are is, of course, a mystery which tasks the imaginations of the thoughtful. Some of George Simenon's best (and saddest) novels are about the tramps of Paris; their lives under the bridges over the River Seine; their fears, conflicts and histories.

These days the tramps are becoming more sophisticated. Several have built small temporary homes out of packing cases and bits and pieces of scrap wood and metal. We saw one with a sofa, a barbecue and a rack for saucepans and crocks neatly stored in a home-made cabinet. We know of at least two tramps who have battery operated portable televisions and we have seen one with a television set, a CD player and a mobile telephone. It was strange to see a tramp texting on a mobile phone while watching his television. (Just how he managed to charge them all is just one of the many Parisian mysteries.) Apart from the tramps with packing cases and small homes the usual clochard's tiny world is defined by the territory he can dominate with a few old flattened out cardboard boxes and a sleeping bag.

If you are (or can arrange to be) in Paris on a Sunday at the end of July then you're in luck. The Tour de France hits Paris at that time of the month and it is, without a shadow of a doubt, the biggest and most spectacular free sporting event in the whole world.

One third of the entire French population stand by the roadside at some point during the three week tour and the man in charge of the tour is reputed to have more power during that three week period than the President of France himself.

Unless you have tickets for the organised seating (which you probably won't have and certainly don't need) the best place to watch Le Tour is either the pavement around the Jardin des Tuileries or the pavement on the north side of the river (the quai des Tuileries) – both these areas are in the 1st.

The cyclists race round the city centre eight or so times and so you get plenty of chances to see them in action. (The snag with watching from the Jardin des Tuileries is that you can't get off what is effectively an island during the race. You have to stay until it's all over, whether you want to or not.)

If you want a place on the Champs-Elysées you'll have to grab yourself a stretch of barrier at about nine o'clock in the morning and stand there, unmoving, for seven or so hours before the cyclists arrive. We don't have the bladders or the patience for that.

The Tour is an extraordinary spectacle. It begins with police cars and motorcycles making sure that the way is clear, then there are the promotional vehicles – cars and lorries from which pneumatic, scantily dressed women toss sweets, maps and coloured caps to the waiting crowds. Some of the promotional vehicles are made in the shape of cakes or cheeses or whatever else seems appropriate to the sponsor.

Then come some of the cars carrying the spare bicycles, together with some press vehicles, more official vehicles, and the breakdown trucks which travel through France with the Tour to pick up any vehicles which might break down. Then there are more cars carrying bicycles. Then more official red cars. (None of the people in these vehicles see any of the race, of course.)

Then comes a gap during which everyone fidgets.

After a few moments police motorcycles come screaming by, far faster than you expect. And then, eventually, the cyclists. You can tell they are coming because the TV company's helicopters, which are relaying the pictures sent from the camera toting motorcycles below, appear overhead.

The cyclists come either in batches or in a long peleton, stretched out and pedalling at nearly 30 mph, just as they have been doing for three weeks. The cyclists are skinny, suntanned and have (literally) not an ounce of fat between them. (They do so much damage to their bodies and immune systems that professional cyclists live, on average, fifteen years less than everyone else.)

The racing cyclists are accompanied by television cameramen on motorcycles (the cameraman riding pillion), press photographers on motorcycles, former tour winners in red cars, travelling with more officials regulating the race, and team cars with spare wheels on the roofs. There is a motorcycle carrying a blackboard to tell the riders what is happening ahead or behind them and a motorcyclist carrying drink bottles so that the domestiques (lesser riders) can carry drinks to their team leaders.

Le Tour is a mobile town of around 3,000 people and it has, for more than a century, been a part of French life. The cyclists keep up a breathtaking pace. They are, by wide acclaim, the fittest sportsmen in the world.

There are thousands of wonderful stories about the Tour.

In the very first Tour de France, held in 1903, the race director took a train to get from Paris to Lyon where the cyclists were headed on the first stage. It was, at the time, the only way for him to get there. Even then, riding boneshaker bicycles, the cyclists got to the destination faster than the train. A cyclist called Maurice Garin (the eventual winner) and some of the others had already started on the next stage by the time the race director got there.

The cyclists today are superhuman but in the old days they were seemingly fearless and beyond pain. In one of the early races a cyclist fell off his bike on rough mountain roads and a piece of flint went into one eye and destroyed it. He wouldn't give up and rode half blind for another two weeks, covering 400 miles a day in what must have been excruciating pain. When he got to Paris doctors removed his damaged eye and found that he also had a broken shoulder and a broken wrist. He rode the following year and on the dusty roads his glass eye became dusty and irritated. He took it out and put cotton wool into the socket. 'I like to pamper myself,' he said, apparently without irony.

The Tour is still tough these days but a century ago it was unbelievable and the rules were sometimes downright cruel. One early cyclist called Eugene Christophe had the misfortune to break a fork on his bicycle. He carried his bicycle on his back for 15 kilometres and eventually found a village forge. He knew he wasn't allowed to have help repairing his bike so he mended it himself. But he was thrown out of the race nevertheless. The race referee ruled that Christophe had broken the rules because the blacksmith had operated the bellows. Christophe was deemed to have accepted outside assistance.

★ ★ ★

You can purchase English newspapers at most of the kiosks in Paris but if you're a magazine junkie and can't manage without your weekly fix then you should visit the Paris branch of W.H. Smith in the rue de Rivoli; a covered cloister-style walkway just a few yards from the place de la Concorde (also in the 1st). W.H. Smith in Paris also sells a marvellous selection of American magazines. For bibliophiles the store stocks a huge variety of English and American paperbacks, often available before they are on the shelves in the UK. They also have a good selection of audio CDs and DVDs though, naturally these, like the books, cost more than they do in the UK. This branch of W.H.Smith is the only one we know of which doesn't sell vast quantities of stationery and greeting cards and it is, in our opinion, much the better for it. It's a proper bookshop.

Another good English bookshop in Paris is Brentano's in the avenue de l'Opera (also in the 1st). Brentano's specialises in American rather than British titles and always has a good selection of books about Paris.

There are numerous other English bookshops in Paris (the best known and most celebrated being, of course, Shakespeare and Co which is in the 5th). Many sell second hand English books as well as new volumes. Gallianos, further along the rue de Rivoli from W.H.Smith, also sells a good range of English books. And the little bookstalls on the quays beside the river often have second hand English books for sale.

2nd Arrondissement

There are a few small shops and one or two fashion houses here, and the arrondissement includes La Bourse and the Bibliothèque National but for us the best part of the 2nd arrondissement are the Passage Jouffroy and the Passage de Panoramas – two beautiful arcades or passageways.

There is no doubt in our mind that the passageways or arcades of Paris are one of the city's best kept and most amazing secrets. We know Parisians who have lived in the city all their lives but who still haven't ever visited them. And we know many regular visitors to Paris who haven't found them either. Inexplicably, many guidebooks ignore them completely.

There are numerous glass-roofed arcades or passages all over the city, most of them dating back to the 19th century or beyond, but the longest, brightest, best and most fun are probably the ones which head north and south from the Boulevard Montmartre in the 2nd arrondissement. The Passage Jouffroy heads north and the Passage de Panoramas goes south. They contain numerous tiny boutiques and cafés and are splendid for browsing on a rainy day. The Jouffroy actually contains its own hotel – the Hôtel Chopin, which has been there since the passage was founded in 1882.

As with most of the other passageways of Paris these two give an exquisite sense of the glory that once was. As you wander about the city you will find numerous other small passageways (especially if you have purchased a proper map to supplement the free one provided by your hotel). Some are quite short, but most are packed with pleasant surprises. The Passage Verdeau (which carries on across the street from the Jouffroy) is packed with fascinating, treasure-trove shops. Other covered arcades and passageways we recommend include the Galerie Vero-Dodat, the Galerie Colbert, the Galerie Vivienne and the Passage de Choiseul.

The 2nd arrondissement also contains the rue St Denis; a famous (or infamous) haunt for prostitutes. If you wander up and down the rue St Denis (even in daylight) you will see streetwalkers advertising their wares on every street corner and in doorways and alleyways. This isn't a street to walk up and down with children, who are likely to want to know why the lady across the road has come out to have a cigarette dressed only in her underwear. The street is also full of bars, peepshows and sex shops.

An old French man who regularly drinks in a café in our street, and who has a bad limp, tells English and American tourists that his infirmity is a result of what he describes as 'an old war wound'. He gets two or three drinks a day on the basis of this, bought for him by sympathetic listeners who wrongly assume that he was injured in the Second World War. But it was a whore wound not a war wound. What his benefactors don't know, and he doesn't mention, is that he got his injury when a whore threw him down the stairs in an establishment just off the rue St Denis. After failing to get his money's worth he had demanded, and been refused, a refund. It was his fault and his responsibility, said the girl.

A word of quiet warning.

Women tourists visiting the rue St Denis (or other such areas of Paris) should dress with care. A female friend of ours called Roberts once complained that she was constantly being harassed by seedy middle aged men. We rushed round to her hotel and found that she was wearing a tight T-shirt with the words 'Roberts Roses Are Bloomin' Marvellous' printed on it in large letters. Her husband and father in law were partners in an eponymous garden centre specialising in roses. What she didn't know was that the words 'Roberts Roses' is, for some reason long ago forgotten, old French slang for breasts. It's perhaps hardly surprising that so many Parisian men in search of comfort mistook the meaning of her advertisement.

You don't have to dress in a whimple and habit but short

skirts, tight tops and lots of flesh might well lead to embarrassing confusion.

3rd Arrondissement

Here you'll find the Musée Picasso (well worth a visit) and a few other, lesser known museums, some of which have excellent exhibitions from time to time (one once held a remarkably uplifting exhibition of bras). The 3rd also contains the Archives Nationales (which we doubt will set your heart aflutter) and some quite smart and fashionable cafés and restaurants which might. (As elsewhere in Paris, restaurants come into and go out of fashion for no discernible reason. Life must be a constant nightmare for restaurateurs. You close the doors early one morning, the King or Queen of Paris, waving goodbye to the great and the good, and the following night you spend an entire evening serving two bowls of soup to a couple from Denmark.)

The bottom end of the arrondissement (looking on the map) contains the Marais. The Marais is the old Jewish quarter of Paris. Although it has in recent years been discovered by property developers and Parisians seeking good value apartments, the Marais still contains a large Jewish population and, as a result, lots of kosher butchers, delicatessens and Jewish restaurants. The area is now mostly restored and is one of the more expensive parts of Paris. If you find yourself on the appropriate corner of the rue de Sevigne peep into the entrance of the Musée Carnavalet and admire the wonderful cobbled courtyard. The Marais is a popular place to wander on a Sunday morning. Most of those wandering are making their way east towards the place des Vosges.

4th Arrondissement

The Centre Pompidou Musée (known to French administrators as the Musée National d'Art Moderne, to locals as the Beaubourg and to tourists as the funny inside-out building that looks as if the builders forgot to take down the scaffolding) and the place des Vosges are in the 4th, as is some of the Marais. The 4th is a busy arrondissement and its two big attractions mean that it attracts huge numbers of tourists.

Secrets of Paris

The Beaubourg, which is the famous or infamous building which has all its piping on the outside, contains one of the world's largest collections of modern and contemporary art. There's some good stuff inside and the special exhibitions are often spectacular. The café on the top floor is pretty good and has wonderful views. The escalators, in their see-through bubbles, are fun to ride. When freshly painted the Beaubourg itself looks either quite jolly or utterly spectacular, depending upon how much you like looking at lots of piping, but when it needs painting (as, sadly, it often seems to do) it looks absolutely gross, more like a scrap dealer's dump than an expensive museum. The colours of the pipes tell anyone who's really interested what they do.

The area around the Beaubourg contains many large cafés which are designed to cater for tourists rather than Parisians and which are, therefore, largely to be avoided unless you feel particularly hungry and really can't manage another step without sustenance. The patch of sloping ground in front of the Beaubourg used to be packed with street entertainers. We've seen fire eaters, jugglers, conjurers, bands and artistes of all kinds appearing there. Sadly, the number of entertainers there has fallen off recently (perhaps because of the French equivalent of health and safety) and the once joyful area is now largely occupied by gangs of motorcyclists who have traded in their motorcycles for large, ferocious looking dogs.

The place des Vosges, a far more classical piece of Paris, contains 36 classic and beautiful 17th century houses with arcades made of stone and brick. The square was inspired by the piazzas of Florence and the central area and the cloisters around it were once a popular place for sporting noblemen to show off their skills with swords of various kinds. The square was originally called place Royale but Napoleon renamed it the place des Vosges in honour of the region of France of that name because it was the first to send him its taxes.

We think the park in the centre of the square is one of the most beautiful small parks in Paris and the cloisters around the square are exquisite. Musicians often play there, particularly at weekends. Sometimes, if you're lucky, you'll find a jazz band playing on one side of the square and a small classical orchestra busking on the other side. It sounds over the top to say it but we'll say it nevertheless: you have never heard music played until you've heard it played in the cloisters of the place des Vosges. Victor Hugo's house, no 6, is dark and rather dull (you'd have to be a real Victor Hugo fan to find it worth a visit and the furniture it contains is pretty dire, though it was here that he wrote Les Miserables – the novel not the musical) but if you go through the nearby alleyway you will find yourself in a secret quadrangle. If you're lucky there will be a solitary violinist playing there. The acoustics are incredible and this is the nearest you'll get to heaven on this earth. Throw a few coins in the violin case.

5th Arrondissement
The 5th contains Notre Dame, at the north edge of the arrondissement. Thanks to Victor Hugo and the eternally famous French fullback Quasimodo, Notre Dame has become one of the most famous churches in the world. (Notre Dame really was in decline until Hugo's best selling novel *The Hunchback of Notre Dame* was published. The church had been badly damaged during the French Revolution when statues which were thought to represent French kings were destroyed. It was Hugo himself who organised a petition which led to restoration of the Gothic masterpiece in the 1820's.) Situated on an island in the middle of the River Seine there is no doubt that it is the most romantically positioned ecclesiastical building in any city (with the possible exception of St Mark's Basilica in Venice) and the gothic design means that Notre Dame looks as attractive in the dull half light of winter as it does in the bright sunshine of summer.

But inside, Notre Dame is a real disappointment. The stained glass is good but the main problem is that the church gets so crowded that any atmosphere which might be there is lost. And those in charge of presenting Notre Dame to the public don't do their legacy any favours by having a gift shop inside the church. We couldn't find the money lenders but they are probably in there, too, somewhere. Tragically, we feel that Notre Dame is a spiritually empty building, full of tourists but empty of atmosphere. The last time we went in there was a service going on but tourists were still flashing away with their cameras. The bottom line is that Notre Dame has about as much spiritual integrity as a chip shop in Birmingham at 11 p.m. on a Saturday night. Bottom line: the outside is well worth a look but the inside is just too disappointing.

In addition to Notre Dame the 5th (also known as the Quartier Latin) contains the Panthéon (a neo-classical necropolis), the Sorbonne (the university founded in 1258), some English language cinemas and a vast number of cafés and stationery shops catering to students. It also contains a great many students.

The area immediately south west of Notre Dame is colourful, charming and great fun and contains some of the biggest student bookshops. The place Saint-Michel is the centre of the area and contains the best cafés. The small alleyways near by, which lead back up towards the boulevard Saint Germain, contain wonderful and colourful and constantly surprising shops. Because the area caters for students as well as tourists the prices (at least in the shops catering to students) tend to be reasonable. This is probably the best place in Paris to buy presents for yourself or for friends. It was these streets which were a source of cobble stones in the 1968 riots. The cobbles were thrown at the police by students. Afterwards the authorities replaced the cobbles with asphalt. It's far more difficult to tear up a chunk of asphalt.

On the Left Bank, almost opposite the Prefecture de Police on the Ile de la Cité (where France's most famous detective, Maigret, sits and puffs at his pipe), you will find the rue du Chat Qui Pêche (named after a cat who used to fish in the cellars when the Seine was high). This is said to be (and we believe it is) the narrowest and shortest thoroughfare in the world. There is only one tiny window looking into the whole street.

While you're in the area around St Michel you must visit the bookshop Shakespeare and Co. It's set back from the riverbank a little way but if you look to your right when you cross the Seine from Notre Dame you'll see it. Named after (but nothing to do with) the wonderful bookshop run by the legendary Sylvia Beech (the bookseller who first published Ulysses by James Joyce, after it was banned in Britain in 1921) Shakespeare and Co is a fascinating treasure-trove of new and second hand books. It was founded in 1951 by George Whitman, a relative of the American poet Walt Whitman. (Like all great men the elder Whitman wanted to be remembered for saying something profound and witty on his death bed. He had allegedly prepared a series of bon mots for his final moment. Whenever he thought he was dying he would utter something deeply moving and yet suitably succinct and memorable. But things didn't go quite according to plan. The last words of Walt Whitman were spoken to his valet Horace Traubel and they were: 'Lift me up, Horace; I want to shit.' Poor fellow. Walt's big mistake was not giving his valet a big tip to lie about the final words.)

George Whitman's inimitable and utterly splendid version of Shakespeare and Co has, over the years, been frequented by Henry Miller, Anaïs Nin, Allen Ginsberg and William Burroughs and it was in his shop that the literary magazine Merlin was founded, later publishing Jean-Paul Sartre, Jean Genet and Samuel Beckett.

St Julien le Pauvre, the church near to Shakespeare and Co, took 300 years to build and generation after generation of carpenters and stone masons worked on the building, keeping the work in the family throughout. The church is set in a pleasant little park which is a good place for a picnic.

On the other side of Shakespeare and Co is the rue de la Huchette – a 13th century street which used to be lined with meat roasters and which is now, appropriately, lined with kebab stalls.

Finally, the 5th also contains the Hôtel Dieu.

The Hôtel Dieu, which was founded by Bishop Landry in AD 561, is the oldest hospital in the world. The Parisian women who looked after patients there probably became the first group of nursing nuns. Today, the Hôtel Dieu is as beautiful as a hospital can be. You can find it on the northern side of the square outside Notre Dame cathedral. Technically, you aren't supposed to go in. (It's not officially open to visitors and, quite naturally, the hospital staff don't want streams of tourists wandering through). But we have tottered in there once or twice. We walked in through the main doors at the front and looked as if we knew what we were doing and should be there (and, most important of all, we didn't look like tourists) and no one stopped us. Inside, the hospital has the most beautiful courtyard surrounded by exquisite cloisters. Doctors may not have been blessed with scanners and several layers of administration when the hospital was built but they knew that fresh air, gentle exercise, bird song and the perfume of flowers made a potent therapeutic mixture and so they built their hospital around a courtyard and provided cloisters where convalescent patients could promenade daily whatever the weather.

There are huge pictures on the walls of the cloisters explaining the history of the place. We stress that the Hôtel Dieu isn't a tourist attraction. It's a working hospital. But we don't think that anyone will object if you go inside to peep at the magnificent cloisters.

The Hôtel Dieu hasn't always been as wonderful as it appears to be today. A report published in 1788, when the Hôtel Dieu had 1,220 beds and was probably the most important hospital in the city, described how patients were crammed between four and six to a bed. Linen and bandages were washed in the Seine which must have been fun for those downstream taking their drinking water from the river.

6th Arrondissement

The 6th arrondissement includes a big chunk of the Quartier Latin and a large part of the area known as St Germain des Prés. It contains the beautiful 12th century St Germain des Prés church and, within hailing distance of it, three of the best known cafés in Paris (Les Deux Magots, Café de Flore and the Brasserie Lipp). The first two are excellent and highly recommended. Brasserie Lipp, though enormously fashionable with politicians, always seems to us to be less friendly, less inviting and the one of the three worth missing. The whole area is thick with excellent cafés and coffee houses. Voltaire, Robespierre, Rousseau and Ben Franklin have all sipped and argued here. Oscar Wilde died beyond his means at No 13 rue des Beaux Arts. His famous final words (much wittier and more often quoted than Mr Whitman's) were: 'Either this wallpaper goes, or I do.' We like to think the wallpaper is still there.

It was in St Germain that Dr Joseph Ignace Guillotine perfected his machine for removing the heads from people while causing them the least amount of pain. (Guillotine was a compassionate man who wanted a painless form of capital punishment as a step towards banning the death penalty, but is, sadly, remembered in a rather different way.) It was also here that the revolutionary politician Marat had his printing press. And just a little way westwards, along the boulevard Saint Germain, you will find, in a small park, a bust on a plinth commemorating Doctor René Théophile Hyacynthe Laennec, the inventor of the stethoscope. Laennec was walking through Paris one day when he noticed a group of children crouched at one end of a hollow wooden log, listening to the sound of a pin being scratched at the other end. (Children had to amuse themselves without television or Play Stations in those days.) Inspired by this simple observation Laennec went home and made a paper tube with which he could listen to his patients' chests without having to lay his head on their bosoms. Thus was the stethoscope born.

The French have a wonderful sense of the absurd and nowhere in Paris is this displayed to more effect than in the pavement just across the square from the St Germain des Prés church. The sculpture there consists of a fountain designed to appear like a burst water main. The paving slabs are fixed as though they have been pushed upwards by the force of water. It's our favourite sculpture in the whole of Paris. Don't miss it.

The 6th also contains the Palais du Luxembourg (now the French Senate) and the Jardin du Luxembourg (the Luxembourg Gardens). The Luxembourg Gardens are exactly what a public garden should be. Mothers and nannies with small children and babies. Old-fashioned green kiosks selling sweets, balloons, coloured windmills and toys. Tennis courts where you can often watch professional quality tennis being played. Games of boules. Men playing chess (whatever the weather). An outdoor table tennis table free for anyone who wants to use it. Flower beds galore. Fountains. Plenty of comfortable chairs and benches. Probably the most colourful and imaginative children's playground in the world. Plenty of places to sit if you want to sunbathe and plenty of places to sit if you prefer the shade. All in all the Jardin du Luxembourg consist of 62 beautiful acres, originally created for Marie de Medicis. In May, orange trees and 200-year-old palms are brought out into the garden for the summer.

7th Arrondissement

Although it looks as though it ought to be a tourist mecca (it contains the Eiffel Tower, the Musée d'Orsay and the Hôtel des Invalides) the 7th is the arrondissement where most of the rich Parisians live. It's home for leading politicians, judges and film stars and also contains more than its fair share of embassies. When you read that such and such a film star lives in Paris, this is probably where they live. The 7th contains some of the best small, specialist food shops, a good many official Government buildings and (because of the embassies, Government buildings and important people who live there) probably more policemen per square yard than any other arrondissement.

The Musée d'Orsay, the arrondissement's biggest and most important museum, was a railway station in the 19th century but has been beautifully converted into a museum dedicated to 19th century and early 20th century art. It may not contain the Mona Lisa or the Venus de Milo but it is, in our view, the best art museum in Paris. It is also home to one of the very best museum cafés in the world. There is a wonderful view of Paris through the glass clock-face. The 7th also contains the Palais-Bourbon (the Assemblée Nationale) which is where the French legislature now sits or stands or sometimes just lolls around; the École Militaire and, in the rue de Babylone, a Japanese style cinema called La Pagode which is possibly quite unlike any cinema ever built in Japan.

But it's the Eiffel Tower which makes the 7th the exciting and attractive arrondissement it is.

The Eiffel Tower, France's 320 metre high national landmark and undoubtedly the most recognised (and reproduced) public erection in the world, was built for the 1889 Paris Exhibition (it took two years to build) and named after Gustav Eiffel who designed it (though he had a lot of skilled engineers helping him). Originally M.Eiffel had a small flat right at the very top of the tower. Until 1930 the Eiffel Tower was the tallest man-made structure in the world.

The Eiffel tower, ultimately graceful and intrinsically feminine in shape and style, was originally built as a sample of the engineers' art and the plan was to demolish it when the lease for the land ran out in 1909. The tower was designed to sway in gales and expand and contract with the temperature. Fortunately for Paris, France and the world the tower wasn't dismantled because it turned out to be useful for sending radio communications around Europe.

Snooty Parisians and snooty tourists turn their noses up at the Eiffel Tower. But we think it is absolutely brilliant. You don't have to buy an Eiffel Tower key ring, ashtray or T-shirt but going up the Tower is one of life's essential experiences and gives a good view of surrounding Paris. (Nearly 200 million people have been up the tower so far.) The big snag is that you have to queue twice. You must queue, at ground floor, to get up to the first or second tier. On the second tier you have to join another queue to get to the top. The last time we went the queue for the lift for the final ride to the top of the tower was (as it often seems to be) about six miles long and we gave up. But a trip to the second stage floor will do just fine. If you're feeling fit and frisky you can walk to the second level. There are 600 steps and in 1905 a man ran up them in three minutes and 12 seconds. If you are hardy enough (and barmy enough) to climb to the top there are 1,665 steps.

From ground level, if you look around the tower you will see the names of all the engineers who helped build it embossed in the ironwork. Occasionally, you'll also see steeple jacks wandering around painting and doing bits and pieces of essential maintenance. Since 1889 the Tower has been repainted 17 times. Each painting uses 50 tonnes of paint and the colour has always varied slightly. Today it has an old bronze polish hue. The tower weighs 10,100 tonnes and is made up of 18,038 pieces of iron and 2,500,000 rivets. (If you don't believe us you're welcome to count them.)

As we've already mentioned one skilful confidence trickster actually managed to sell the tower several times to gullible Americans who thought they could take it back to liven up their back gardens.

Over the years the Eiffel Tower has been used in many imaginative ways. During the First World War, for example, the French put trained parrots onto the Tower in the hope that the birds would give advance warning of incoming aircraft and enable anti-aircraft gunners to shoot them down. (The planes, not the birds). The plan was abandoned when the French realised that the parrots couldn't discriminate between Allied aircraft and German aircraft and that although they were very good at announcing the imminent arrival of the 11.43 from Berlin they were unable to differentiate between that and the 11.43 from Lyon.

At night the Eiffel Tower is floodlit. The lighting is exquisite. We think the Tower looks at its best after dark. Concerts are often held around the base of the Tower and these attract large audiences (and absolutely huge audiences if they involve Johnny Hallyday). The Tower is often used as a backcloth for spectacular firework displays.

The Hôtel des Invalides, another attraction in the 7th, is also well floodlit (the French do floodlighting and fireworks better than anyone in the world) though the golden dome means that it looks even more dramatic in the daylight – particularly if the sun is shining. It gleams and sparkles in the slightest bit of sunshine.

You should make sure that you allow plenty of time for visiting the Hôtel des Invalides. Built in the 17th century by Louis XIV as a convalescent home and hospice for injured soldiers, the Hôtel des Invalides is now best known as the final resting place of Napoleon Bonaparte. (He was moved there, from St Helena, in 1861 and the gravestone from his St Helena resting place now lies in one of the smaller courtyards).

Apart from taking a peek at Napoleon's extraordinary tomb underneath the gold domed majesty (the cupola is covered in gold leaf and worth a fortune if you could scrape it all off) there are two museums. The Musée de l'Armee and the Musée des Plans-Reliefs. The former is well worth a visit and the latter is well worth a miss unless you're dedicated to studying Plans-Reliefs. In the army museum, it is mind boggling to see the length of some of the early rifles which were used. The guns were so long that some poor devil had to stand at the business end and hold it up while the chap several yards away pulled the trigger. The poor soldier holding up the business end invariably went deaf. At the very least.

And do take a slow wander around the first floor cloisters which surround the main cobbled courtyard of the Hôtel des Invalides. (The Hôtel des Invalides contains over a dozen courtyards). You get there by ascending the staircases at either Gate J or Gate G at the southern end of the courtyard (the Cour d'Honneur). There is a Renault tank from 1915 at the foot of the staircase at Gate J.

The small doors on the cloistered landing originally led to the rooms in which the wounded soldiers lived out their final days. Today, sadly, the doors are all sealed up and the rooms have become part of the museum. Imagine, as you walk, Napoleon's old guard, hobbling round, chatting about the snows in Moscow and their leader's extraordinary return from Elba. Stand and look out over the cobbled courtyard, lean on the stone wall where a thousand arms have leant before, and, with a little imagination, you will be able to hear the clatter of horses' hooves. At the southern end, above the soldiers' church, you can see a statue of Napoleon, gazing out on his imaginary troops. At the northern end there is one of the most wonderfully complex sundials we've ever seen.

The Hôtel des Invalides was, as the name suggests, originally a convalescent home for wounded soldiers and whatever the weather they would take their daily constitution in the cloisters. The steps up to the cloisters are shallow and wide to make it easier for wounded one-legged soldiers to get up and down them. If you look carefully at the pillars around the cloisters you can still see bits of very early graffiti of the 'Kilroy was here' type carved into the stone. We've seen inscriptions marked 1719, 1746, 1760, 1776 and 1789. Several old soldiers marked out the months and years they spent in the Hôtel des Invalides, for all the world as though they were prisoners.

To the French, Napoleon Bonaparte is not just the greatest French hero, he is the greatest man the world has ever known. When you realise that, so far, there have been over 45,000 books about him published, it's difficult to argue with them. Napoleon was responsible for just about everything that is good about modern

France. After establishing a military dictatorship in 1799 (he was just 30-years-old at the time, which must make the rest of us chronic under-achievers) he introduced the Napoleonic Code (still in place and the basis of the legal system which the French use and which is now being used throughout the European Union), reconstructed the French education system, built many of the most useful and most famous roads (not personally you understand, he was too slight a figure to be of much use with a shovel, but he planned their routes and gave the orders for their building), planned most of the modern city of Paris and eventually found time to crown himself emperor in 1804.

After a short enforced holiday on the island of Elba, Napoleon escaped, re-gathered his army and made himself Emperor again. (The story of how he did this – turning the army sent to arrest him into his own bodyguard – is one of the most amazing in history.) He looked after his relatives (he put members of his family on thrones all over Europe) but he also looked after his soldiers. French roads are lined with tall trees because Napoleon wanted the trees there to provide future generations of soldiers with some shade (he was accustomed to ordering his soldiers to march constantly from one battle to another).

The irony is – and we recommend that you don't mention this to a French citizen unless you deliberately want to upset him or her because they tend to be a bit touchy about it – but Napoleon nearly wasn't French at all. He was born in 1769 on the island of Corsica and his parents were Italian. Corsica only became a province of France in 1768. Close call.

(Three of the most famous 'Frenchmen' of all time were Napoleon, Simenon and Picasso. Napoleon was born on Corsica, Simenon (the creator of Maigret) was born in Belgium and Picasso was born in Spain. Only one of the three was actually French and he only just made it.)

Napoleon died on St Helena (French nationalists, of whom there are a growing number, have never forgiven the British for killing Joan of Arc or for sending Napoleon so far away from home) and it wasn't until years later that it was considered safe to move him to the Hôtel des Invalides. (His miraculous escape from Elba had left everyone feeling rather nervous. The French and British Governments presumably wanted to be sure that if they brought him back to Paris he wasn't going to jump out of his coffin and back onto his white horse. Even when they got him back they still weren't entirely comfortable with having him so close to the seat of power. Napoleon's corpse is wrapped in a nest of six beautifully crafted wood and metal coffins, intended, we suspect, more to prevent him getting out and starting any more wars than to stop anyone stealing the body. There are iron bars across the windows too.)

Everyone who visits the Hôtel des Invalides gets to learn much the same about the great French Emperor. Everyone knows he was a Brigadier General at 24 and that he was beaten by Nelson in the Battle of the Nile and at Trafalgar. Everyone knows he was beaten by Wellington at Waterloo.

So here's a fact that not many people know (and which doesn't appear in the usual guidebooks).

Napoleon's penis was cut off by the physician who performed the autopsy. It is now said to look a bit like a grape. It was put up for sale at a famous London auction house in 1972 where it failed to reach the reserve price. We are afraid that we have no idea where it is now but if you see Napoleon's penis on offer on a market stall (and it comes with a decent and convincing history) we suggest you snap it up; it could be worth a fortune to a collector.

If you want to see how a thriving city has managed to overcome all the problems put in its way by supermarkets and European bureaucrats then, while you are in Paris, you should visit the sort of area where real Parisians do their daily shopping. One of the best and most accessible is the rue Cler in the 7th arrondissement, midway between the Hôtel des Invalides and the Eiffel Tower.

We recommend the rue Cler because it is a typical, traditional French shopping street. It's a shopping precinct which contains bakers, florists, greengrocers, an ironmonger, a Post Office, a bookshop, cheese shops, restaurants and so on. Traffic is officially barred but the French don't take much notice of inconvenient rules like this and so you do need to watch out for cars, vans and motorcycles. Politicians and show business stars who live in the area do their shopping here. There are four or five supermarkets in rue Cler or on the streets nearby but the small, specialist shops aren't just surviving, they are thriving. So, for example, you will find one shop selling nothing but different types of olive oil and another selling nothing but vacuum cleaners.

(Specialist shops do well in Paris. In the Marais we know of a shop selling absolutely nothing but white blouses and another selling nothing but jewellery made from amber. There are of course plenty of shops selling nothing but cheeses (General de Gaulle once asked how anyone could be expected to govern a country with 325 different cheeses but things have moved on since the General's day and the French now have over 500 different types of home grown cheese) and others selling only red meat, pig meat or poultry. A Parisian housewife who eschews supermarkets and want to get the ingredients for a stew or a steak and kidney pie could take a day doing her shopping.)

Singer/songwriter Serge Gainsbourg was one of the many stars who lived in the 7th and if you want to visit his former home the address is 5 rue de Verneuil in the 7th. Gainsbourg was famous for three things. First, his record *Je t'aime,* made with Jane Birkin, was banned but famously got to number 1 in the British pop charts. Second, Gainsbourg was famous for burning a 500 franc note on television to prove that he was rich. Finally, Gainsbourg produced a successful but rather controversial reggae version of la Marseillaise. Most shops still sell postcards of the singer/songwriter unshaven, with a glass of Pernod in front of him and a cigarette in one hand. Serge Gainsbourg was one of the French show business celebrities treated as royalty. His daughter is now a star. (As is Johnny Hallyday's son.)

As you wander around here, as elsewhere, keep a look out for shops labelled 'Depot Vente'. These are second hand stores where Parisians take their unwanted furniture and paraphernalia and leave it for sale, paying a commission to the owner of the store. The prices of unsold items fall over time, and if you fancy something and are staying in Paris long enough you can wait around until the price falls to what you are prepared to pay.

Finally, in the 7th, we recommend that you visit St Clothilde. The French are not great church goers; on the whole they prefer to sit and eat rather than kneel and pray and since they eat out a lot they don't need to go to church to find an excuse to buy (or show off) a new hat. But, as a hangover from holier times, Paris is full of churches. The only one in Paris which we suggest you actually go inside is the neo-Gothic St Clothilde (to be found in the 7th, in between the rue St Dominique and the rue de Grenelle, and surrounded by French Ministries.) The church organ is much admired by those who admire church organs.

The real beauty of St Clothilde is that it is the most spiritual church we've ever been into. To put it in perspective, St Clothilde is the only church where either of us has ever lit a candle. And every time we visit (which is often) we light candles in memory of lost friends, relatives or animals. You can't buy souvenirs, crucifixes and so on in St Clothilde but there is more peace and spiritual contentment to be found there than in any other church we have ever visited. It is the holiest of holy places.

8th Arrondissement

The spectacular but (from a shopping point of view rather over-rated) Champs-Elysées runs right down the middle of the 8th arrondissement. The newspaper kiosks on the pavement on both sides of the Champs-Elysées sell English magazines as well as newspapers. Other points of interest include the Gare St Lazare (in front of which there stands a magnificent clock sculpture which is well worth seeing if you're in the area), the Parc de Monceau (one of the poshest and in our view least friendly parks in Paris), the place de la Concorde and l'Eglise de la Madeleine. There are some very expensive art galleries and some hugely overpriced cafés and restaurants in the 8th arrondissement and Fauchon, Paris's most upmarket grocery (even the potatoes look as if they've been to the beauticians) is on the place de la Madelaine behind the church. (When Parisian students rioted in 1968 and wanted windows to break they headed straight for Fauchon, proving that even revolutionaries have a taste for the best.) The 8th also contains the Grand Palais and the Petit Palais which were built for the 1900 World Exhibition (and which are now still used to house exhibitions) and the Palais de l'Elysée which is the residence of the French President.

Around the place de la Concorde, as elsewhere in the city, you will, if you walk through the city, notice many plaques commemorating the resistance fighters who died defending their city during the German occupation of the Second World War. Pale beige plaques, some carrying the words 'Ici est tombé' (Here fell) are dotted everywhere. We counted ten around this, the world's biggest roundabout. With additionally poignant tragedy, these ten died during the last minutes of the occupation. The leader of the German command, Dietrich von Choltitz, defied Hitler's orders to destroy Paris and refused to give the order to tell his men to ignite the explosives that had been planted under all of the city's landmarks, including Notre Dame and the Eiffel Tower. But he did tell his men to fight until the last cartridge. And they did just that. One French tank commander, Pierre Laigle, having just made his way into Paris, stopped to find a telephone from which to ring the fiancée he hadn't seen or heard from in four years. She set off to find him but before she could get to him a German sniper, hiding in the Ministère de la Marine, shot and killed him. Two Red Cross workers, both wearing distinctive arm bands, were shot dead while carrying the wounded to safety in those last hectic minutes.

Also in the 8th there is the Paris stamp market.

Even if you don't collect stamps (or know anyone who does) the Paris stamp market (held in the avenue Gabriel close to the Rond Point des Champs-Elysées, at the bottom of the Champs-Elysées) is well worth visiting. The best day to go is Thursday, and the market is open all day whatever the weather. Even today the market is indistinguishable from the one which starred, together with Cary Grant, Audrey Hepburn and Walter Matthau in *Charade* (the 1963 film, directed by Stanley Donen.) Cary and Audrey are looking for something valuable when they suddenly realise that the 'something' they are looking for is a mouldy old stamp stuck on an envelope and that the stamp is worth about fifty zillion pounds.

In addition to stamps many of the market stalls specialise in selling old postcards and letters. The French are very keen on collecting postcards and you can buy all sorts of fascinating old cards from the early 20th and late 19th centuries. The prices here are extremely reasonable and you can pick up a mid 19th century letter (complete with stamp) for hardly anything. The last time we were there we bought a fistful of letters and old bills from the middle part of the 19th century and paid just a few euros for them. They're fun to have and to read. We have even managed to buy (again, very cheaply) letters sent out before the French cottoned on to the idea of using postage stamps.

If you want postcards that are a bit out of the ordinary to send to friends you can find unused old cards here too. And one or two of the stalls will even sell you cut price, useable stamps to put on your cards. (The dealers buy them from collectors who bought sheets of stamps hoping that they would go up in value but then, after a decade of disappointment, sold them at a discount to their face value.)

A man who runs one of the stalls on the stamp market told us a truly sad story.

In 1980, West Germany printed stamps to commemorate the 1980 Olympic Games in Moscow. However, after the USSR's invasion of Afghanistan, West Germany withdrew from the games in protest and destroyed the stamps they had printed before issuing them. But the German Minister of Posts, a Herr Gscheidle, kept a sheet of the stamps in a drawer, suspecting, perhaps, that the stamps would one day be valuable and might make a useful pension fund. If that was his intention, he was right for one of the stamps was subsequently sold for 74,000 Deutschmarks. Sadly, however, it wasn't sold by Herr Gscheidle. His wife, keen on entering postal competitions, had found the sheet of stamps in a drawer and had used them on her letters.

The 8th arrondissement is also where you will find the avenue Montaigne.

If you want to see what the fashion houses of Paris are currently offering the avenue Montaigne is, without a doubt, the best street in Paris to visit. Actually, it is the most complete fashion street on the planet since it is reputed to contain more de luxe labels and couturiers than Madison avenue in New York, Bond street in London or the via Montenapoleone in Milan. To the rich and fashion conscious the avenue Montaigne, the avenue George V and rue François 1er form Paris's 'triangle d'or' (golden triangle).

Even if you find the whole fashion business nauseatingly self-indulgent, and painfully superficial, it's well worth going there just for a good laugh. Here you will find Dior, Chanel, Prada, Jimmy Choo, Ungaro, Valentino, Chloé, Nina Ricci, Celine, Bottega Veneta, Armani, Louis Vuitton, Uncle Tom Cobbleigh and many, many more familiar names. (As an aside, it is worth remembering that haute couture in Paris was founded by an Englishman called Charles Frederick Worth. Mr Worth was invited to design clothes for the wife of Napoleon III, Empress Eugenie, and to protect his designs he founded the Chambre Syndicale de la Haute Couture. The world of fashion, like football, tennis, cricket and rugby is an English invention.)

Designing frocks is not an art, it is a craft with airs and graces but in Paris, as everywhere else, the people who work in the fashion industry like to think of themselves as heroes battling in the war against yesterday's clothes. They have succeeded in convincing themselves that they are artists. (In reality, of course, they are no more artists than are the people who design bathtubs or cars.)

Nowhere in the world do fashion designers and models have a greater opinion of themselves than in Paris. You would think they were all finding cures for cancer or working for global peace. Models (men and women who have acquired the enormous skill of being able to walk in a straight line while wearing clothes) are feted as though they are astronauts or sporting heroes. We love these people. They are so false and full of airs that it is a bizarre joy to watch them at work.

Our favourite pastime here is to wander along the avenues, looking in the shop windows, spotting celebrities with the paparazzi and trying to find the most absurdly overpriced item on sale. Shoes and pitifully tiny handbags at £1,000 each are commonplace. Last time we visited we discovered an utterly absurd looking jacket for just under £20,000. It was made out of various bits of dead animal and no ordinary mortal would have given it a second look if it had been on the £1 rack in a local charity shop. Marvellous.

Our second favourite pastime is watching fat American tourists hobbling out of one of the exclusive stores clutching a large, expensive, heavily branded carrier bag containing an example of the couturier's latest nightmare in silk. Just how often these flimsy and often revealing creations get worn back in Texas or Delaware is something of a mystery. The stores claim that their target customers are young, rich, royals. In their dreams. In reality (admittedly, an alien concept in the world of fashion), their customers are overweight commodities traders from Hong Kong, the haughty mistresses of Russian Mafia hoods and the rotund, waddling wives of store owners from Pennsylvania.

Hang around this district long enough and eventually you will probably be approached by a Japanese tourist wanting you to wander into Louis Vuitton and buy bags and things for them. The scam, a sort of luggage arbitrage, is something to do with the fact that Louis Vuitton bags sold in Tokyo cost more than they do in Paris. To take advantage of this discrepancy, gangs of buyers totter into the store with armfuls of euros and stagger out with armfuls of bags. Or at least they would if they were allowed to. And that's where you come in. Because the store is now wise to this perfect example of capitalism in action, and has apparently put a limit on the number of items Japanese tourists can buy, the buyers try to find tourists to go in and do their shopping for them. They give you a fistful of euros and a shopping list. You come out, after having enjoyed a shopping blitz at someone else's expense, and hand over the goodies. A bit like a Chinese meal, we suppose. Satisfying at the time but not really rewarding in the long run. We should warn you that since buying handbags on someone's behalf is now undoubtedly illegal this is probably a scam you should avoid. We can't see the French police sending you to Devil's Island for taking part. But why risk it?

Two famous nightclubs, The Lido and the Crazy Horse Saloon, are both to be found in the 8th. There are many others too.

When Elvis Presley was posted to Germany he came to Paris every weekend and was a keen aficionado of traditional Paris night life. It is said that he deflowered all the famous Bluebell girls. Miss Bluebell was apparently very proud that all the girls she employed were virgins. But Elvis got to them. You might expect the French to have been slightly peeved by this – particularly in view of their low opinion of Americans. But, on the contrary, the French tell this story with great pride. First, because it shows that there were once lots of virgins in Paris. And second because it was Elvis Presley who deflowered them.

9th Arrondissement

The 9th arrondissement contains many of the city's biggest and best shops. It also contains the beautiful Opera Garnier (the original Paris Opera House) which was commissioned by Napoleon III, designed by Garnier and opened in 1875.

From the outside, the old Paris Opera House is breathtaking. It dominates La place de l'Opera (as it was no doubt intended to do) and the steps up to the front entrance are a regular meeting place for students, tourists and people who are lost, want a sit down and can't afford the prices in the excellent Café de la Paix across the road. (The Café de la Paix is one of the great Parisian cafés. It's where the Parisians go to meet friends or to rest their feet after a few hours hard work in the Galeries Lafayette. Food and drink is expensive but, remember, you're not buying sustenance; you're renting a seat from which you can watch the world go by.)

On the outside, the Opera House has a magnificent gold dome which glitters in the sunshine. Inside it has a spectacularly colourful ceiling. Long before anyone had the idea of building an inside out museum in the Marais, or putting a huge glass pyramid in the Louvre courtyard some brave soul had the idea of inviting Marc Chagall to paint the ceiling of the Paris Opera House. Chagall's fantastic imagination and use of colour made him the perfect choice for the job but it is difficult to think of any city in the world where such an artist would have been given his head in such an important and historic building. The result is breathtaking and well worth a look.

The 9th is also the home of the Drouot, the biggest auction house in the world. The Drouot fills a block between the rue Drouot and the rue Chauchat and has been doing business since June 1st 1852. There are 17 auction rooms and sooner or later everything in France passes through its doors and under the ivory hammers of the Drouot auctioneers. In 1990 they sold a piece of the Eiffel Tower's staircase. In 1991 they sold Rimbaud's passport. In 1914 they sold a collection of paintings which included ten Matisses, 12 Picassos and works by van Gogh, Dufy and Gauguin. The whole lot went for just 100,000 francs. They sell two million items a year and hold 2,000 auctions.

10th Arrondissement

The 10th is the home of two large railway stations: the Gare du Nord and the Gare de l'Est. These two stations sit right next to one another and their names denote the areas of France which they serve rather than their position in the city. Apart from these two large stations (and an enormous number of cafés, restaurants and bistros catering to travellers) this is not an arrondissement of great interest. It is, to be honest, a rather cheap and scruffy area and is not a fair introduction to the wonderful city of Paris. The 10th does also contain the Canal Saint Martin which has a certain traditional, rustic charm and is a magnet for people who love canals.

11th Arrondissement

The best thing we can think to say about the 11th is that Simenon's fictional detective Inspector Maigret is supposed to live in the boulevard Richard Lenoir. Since Maigret doesn't actually exist and, therefore, doesn't actually live there, that probably tells you all you need to know about the 11th. The 11th arrondissement does contain the Bastille, which sounds like a very impressive building but is now the place de la Bastille or, more accurately, a large traffic island. The Bastille was originally part of Paris's defenses but was turned into a jail and it is now famous (and an integral part of French history) because the people of Paris stormed the building on 14th July 1789 (a day now known as Bastille Day) and started the French Revolution.

On the day the Bastille was stormed, the entry in Louis XVI's diary entry was confined to one word: 'Rien'. That, of course, probably helps explain why they stormed the Bastille in the first place.

12th Arrondissement

The place de la Bastille is at the north west corner of the 12th arrondissement, which contains the Gare du Lyon and the new Paris opera house (the Opera Bastille). Of the two the Gare du Lyon is by far the most attractive and most functional. The now not so new Opera house looks to us as though it was approved by committees who regard beauty as a betrayal and minimalism as a doctrine. A plague on all their opera houses, say we.

There is a marble plaque screwed to a wall of an elegant building on the rue Sidi-Brahim in the 12th arrondissement which reads: 'Le 17 Avril 1967 ici il ne c'est rien passe'. (Nothing much happened here on 17th April 1967).

How can anyone fail to love such a city?

The 12th also contains many parks and a 2,300 acre wood known as the Bois de Vincennes. This may sound cruel but we can't imagine why you would want to go to the 12th unless you want to catch a train from the Gare du Lyon.

13th Arrondissement

The 13th arrondissement sits neatly between the 12th and the 14th. It contains the Gare d'Austerlitz and a lot of buildings. Keep away. You would have more fun in the 12th and you know what we think of that. Actually, you would probably have more fun in Wolverhampton.

14th Arrondissement

By far the biggest attraction in the 14th is the Cimetière du Montparnasse and that probably tells you everything you want to know about the 14th. Maupassant, Samuel Beckett, Serge Gainsbourg, Jean-Paul Sartre and Simon de Beauvoir are buried here, as, indeed, are a lot of other people. It's the second biggest and second most interesting cemetery in Paris. The 14th also contains the Catacombes, wherein you will find the bones of several million skeletons. This is underground and, is therefore, a good place to go if it's raining and you want to look at old bones.

15th Arrondissement

The Montparnasse Tower (Paris's only skyscraper building) stands right in the northernmost corner of the 14th, where it meets the 6th (just above it in the spiral) and the 15th (just to the left). Technically, the Tower is in the 15th. It glitters like a huge gold ingot when the sun is shining and was built so that the French could show the world that they could make a high rise building if they wanted to. We think it's far more attractive from a distance than it is close up. Inside it is boring.

The 15th is on the wrong side of the Eiffel Tower and is a fashionable area for living in. It is popular with those who can't afford a place in the 7th. It's more fun than it looks. There are no great attractions here but the area just south of the Champ de Mars (the gardens which stretch down below the Eiffel Tower) is worth a wander.

There are many hotels here (most of them of the cheaper variety) but unless you are prepared to do a lot of travelling the 15th arrondissement is simply too far out of very central Paris. A hotel closer to the heart may be a little more expensive but in the long run you'll save money and time by choosing more central accommodation.

16th Arrondissement

The 16th arrondissement includes the Bois de Boulogne (2,137 acres of woods, lawns, lakes, parks, racecourses and quite a few prostitutes of various types touting for business) and the enormously and curiously impressive Jardin du Trocadero and the Palais de Chaillot. The Palais de Chaillot includes a theatre, a film library and the Museum of French Monuments, which we heartily recommend to anyone who finds Paris too exciting and needs to doze for a while.

Right across the river from the Eiffel Tower, and stretching up to the Arc de Triomphe, the 16th is a pleasant enough place to live for people who need lots of space, but is too full of offices and dull buildings to be much fun for the flâneur.

17th Arrondissement

Many fashionable guidebooks recommend the numerous flea markets (Marchés aux Puces) which exist in Paris. Many are found in the Parisian outskirts. One of the biggest is on the far edge of the 17th. 'You must go,' gush the guidebook writers with unstoppable enthusiasm. 'Wander past quaint market stalls in hidden parts of Paris and discover bargains galore in the way the Parisians do.' They give complicated instructions on how to find your way to these markets, which are invariably held in some dreary and unloved suburb of the city.

When you get there you will almost certainly be disappointed.

There may well have been some bargains available a few decades ago but these days a trip to a Parisian flea market will prove to be about as rewarding (in every sense of the word) as an extended tour of the Roissy airport. You will occasionally find stalls flogging bits and pieces of tatty second hand furniture (though you would be wise to consider how you're going to get your double wardrobe back to whence you came before you hand over your money) but these days most of the stalls in the flea markets sell leather jackets (not much more expensive than you can buy them in a store), CDs, DVDs (which may well not work on your machine when you get them home) and hot dogs (which, if you eat one, will probably result in you spending the rest of your trip firmly fixed to your hotel lavatory). The stall holders and barkers are French but a hefty proportion of the customers are American, German, Japanese, Chinese, Dutch, Russian and British – all of whom will be carrying their own copies of the same damned guidebooks which put them onto the place. Go to a flea market early in the morning at a weekend (as is usually recommended) and you will find yourself one of a crowd of tourists. The Parisians are not so stupid as to bother going. They are tucked up at home; in bed with a bag of croissants, a pot of coffee and the newspapers.

Apart from flea markets there are some railway lines in the 17th. And some shops, houses and offices. We cannot think of any reason why you would want to go to the 17th unless you had been tricked into staying in a hotel there. We did see a claim in one guidebook that the view from the Conference Centre is quite good but we happily confess that we haven't checked this out. If you are reduced to trying out this view then you have probably been in Paris too long and should try Venice or Amsterdam for a while.

18th Arrondissement

The 18th contains the ghosts of artists such as Picasso, Matisse and Utrillo. It also contains the Sacre Coeur and the place du Tetre, the Cimetière de Montmartre (the third biggest and third most impressive and third most interesting cemetery in Paris – which contains, among others, what's left of Degas, Stendhal, Berlioz and François Truffaut) and miles and miles of fascinating little alleyways and passageways. This is the part of Paris for which the word 'picturesque' was invented. Steep winding streets. Stone steps. Metal handrails. Wonderful small restaurants. Smoky bars. Tiny hotels with rice paper partitions. It is the part of Paris that contains all those long stone staircases so loved by photographers using black and white film (mainly because, at the time, there wasn't any colour film available, and weren't they lucky).

In the daytime, the 18th is a busy, working class area which also caters for tourists who want to visit and photograph the extraordinary and timeless beauties of Montmartre; the home territory of Toulouse-Lautrec and Renoir, the Moulin Rouge, the can-can and mind-rotting absinthe.

Sacre Coeur is dismissed by the sort of people who think pickled sheep are art as looking too much like a wedding cake. Ignore these deadheads. Sacre Coeur, in the heart of Montmartre, and on the northern edge of Paris, dominates the northern skyline of Paris and it is staggeringly beautiful. The pavement in front of Sacre Coeur provides the very best panoramic view of Paris.

In addition to being one of the best known, Sacre Coeur is truly one of the most stunning churches in Europe. Yes, it looks like a wedding cake. (Or, rather, wedding cakes look like Sacre Coeur.) But, what's so wrong with that?

Sacre Coeur was built in celebration of the bloody repression of the Paris commune and it was built on a part of Paris called La Butte Montmartre which bears an uncanny resemblance to a block of one of those varieties of cheese which are full of holes. The biggest and most famous hill in Paris is honeycombed with caves, tunnels and disused galleries left over after centuries of quarrying for the stone and gypsum (the original Plaster of Paris) with which much of the city was built. (There is a saying known throughout France that 'there is more of Montmartre in Paris than there is of Paris in Montmartre'. For over twenty years deep cracks have been appearing in the walls of houses in Montmartre and buildings have slipped. At least one area has had to be evacuated. Tourist buses rolling through the narrow, twisting streets have created thousands of tiny earthquakes and have constantly widened existing fissures. There are houses where drawers slide open if they aren't jammed shut. Architects and engineers agree that is only the crust of buildings on the surface which holds the area together – and above ground. Every now and again there are rumours that the whole area will fall down and disappear into a big hole in the ground, with just the dome of Sacre Coeur sticking out. (There are also rumours that other parts of Paris are riddled with termites. It is said that when the termites all stop holding hands vast amounts of valuable real estate will disappear.)

Inside, Sacre Coeur isn't anything special and even the most enthusiastic students of church interiors can safely give it a miss. But the outside is spectacular and, unlike many sightseeing specialities, looks just as good close up as it does on postcards. And, we repeat, the views from the pavement, steps and gardens in front of and below Sacre Coeur are sensational. The word majestic is no exaggeration here.

There always seem to be Algerian tinkers flogging native masks and bits of leather work on the steps. Their goods are all laid out on rugs and if a policeman is seen approaching you'll see why. They simply pull together the four corners of their rug and scarper. Most of these guys could win Olympic middle distance medals for sprinting while carrying a large heavy rug full of tat.

Occasionally, there will be a busker in the vicinity. On different occasions we've seen a violinist, a cellist, a string quartet and a saxophonist. The acoustics are brilliant and everything sounds dreamy. A tone deaf man playing the tambourine would probably sound good.

Behind Sacre Coeur lies the place du Tetre.

In the old days this was an artists' hang out. These days it's a hang out for tourists. But it's colourful and enormous fun and quite pretty and although art snobs will turn up their noses at the paintings on sale you aren't going there as an art critic; you're going there because it's fun and unforgettable. It's fairground fun.

There are restaurant tables in the centre of the square and artists working at easels all the way around them. Some of the artists are excellent, some are very good and some are neither. Their plan, obviously, is to sell their paintings to the tourists and they seem to do quite well. You won't be surprised to see that most of the pictures seem to be of Paris, though there are the usual bowls of fruit and a clowns. If you walk right round the square you will be approached at least a dozen times by young sketch artists wanting to do your portrait in charcoal, chalk or crayons. Just smile and shake your head if you're not interested. There are plenty of other potential customers so they won't hassle you. Some of the artists do straightforward portraits and some do cartoons. Just make sure you know what you're getting before you sit down on the little canvas stool.

There are tourists who visit Sacre Coeur by taxi. This is a huge mistake. Get there on foot. Take the metro to the Abbesses station and walk up the steps to Sacre Coeur on the top of the hill. Or, better still, walk up from the place de l'Opera. It's a long climb but well worth it. (There is a funicular railway alongside the steps up to Sacre Coeur for those who really can't face the final climb.) If you don't walk you will miss the feel of the place. And, anyway, you haven't been to Montmartre unless you've climbed up or down one of the many sets of steep stone steps which lead up to the top of the hill.

At night the whole area changes dramatically. This is the home of many of Paris's most famous nightclubs, strip clubs and sex shops.

Glamour, excitement, bright lights − Montmartre has it all.

Every building seems to contain either a restaurant, a café, a theatre or a nightclub. After dark the pavements lower down in Montmartre are packed with pimps and prostitutes and every street corner and every doorway is a neatly defined (and jealously guarded) sales territory for someone selling something you wouldn't ever see advertised on TV or on a street side hoarding but which is, nevertheless, a version of the most popular commodity in the world: sex.

Walk slowly along the boulevard de Clichy, or one of the streets running into it, and every few steps your journey will be interrupted by slender young men in suits and open necked shirts who will ooze out of the darkness with big white smiles and casual, throw away invitations which probably break most known laws. They wear their hair dark and oily and chain-smoke French untipped cigarettes.

The doorways which aren't occupied by slender young men in suits are occupied by young women dressed, whatever the weather, in nothing very much at all. Thigh-high boots, fishnet stockings, suspender belts, spike heels, micro skirts, hot pants, plunge tops revealing seemingly bottomless cleavage canyons, skintight leather catsuits, shoulder length wigs in the most startling colours, unbuttoned blouses and skirts with slits up to the waist.

By daybreak the young men in suits are at home in bed, or in their favourite café playing cards, boasting, gambling and spending their illegal earnings. (Theoretically, gambling is illegal in France. Napoleon Bonaparte outlawed gambling and it has been against the law ever since. The only exceptions are State-run gambling activities – such as the lottery and the State-run casinos – which are, of course, entirely legal.) The lights are off and the clubs seem to have mysteriously disappeared. The streets from which they operated are now cluttered with empty bottles, litter and other debris. The area seems full of Arab cake shops and shoe shops. Grey walls are decorated with peeling posters and spattered with colourful, indecipherable graffiti. The only reminder that this is the sex quarter of the romantic capital of the world comes from the fact that a few of the street corners and some of the doorways are still occupied by prostitutes. The girls who are working the day shift are bolder and more obvious than their night shift sisters. They lean openly against lamp posts or they patrol their stretch of pavement, swinging their hips and parading their wares aggressively and unselfconsciously. The street walkers of the day tend to be a different breed to their sisters of the night. They are usually older, considerably plumper and rounder, and probably a good deal cheaper too. They are more brazen; bare breasts and skirts slit right to the waist, revealing stocking tops and suspenders, show that these women are catering to a different market.

The night girls, more flamboyant, more exotic, better made-up, and more expensive cater to the tourists. They cater to the imagination; to those seeking something special.

The women who work the day shift cater largely to the locals who know exactly what they want and don't want to pay a fortune for presentation. The day shift workers cater to men who want to satisfy a simple, unromantic, unexciting physical need. The night girls are titillating. The day girls are simply provocative; the fast food providers of the Parisian sex industry.

The French have always been known for their open attitude towards sex. It is sometimes said that in the distant, bygone days, when courting French couples had to be accompanied by a chaperon, the chaperon was there not to stop the couple having sex but to give instructions, advice, encouragement and applause (and to be able to give a full report to everyone later).

Prostitution, in its various forms of professionalism, has a long history in France. Innkeepers in France used to routinely ask visiting males whom they knew to be strangers if they wanted a room 'sans ou avec'; meaning with or without a woman. In central France, for example, it was assumed that any man from the north of the country would have travelled a long way and would, consequently, be lonely, cold and in need of comfort.

A century or so ago it was not unknown for women with husbands in the army to send their spouses money so that they could regularly buy a clean woman whenever one was available.

A few decades ago the brothels in Paris were shut down by authorities who hoped that by doing this they would be able to bring an end to prostitution. All that happened, of course, was that the girls went onto the streets. In the brothels the girls had regular medical examinations and carried certificates showing that they were healthy. On the streets there were no medical examinations and no certificates and the incidence of venereal disease rocketed. That was the sole consequence of the authorities' decision to close the brothels: an increase in the incidence of disease.

Today, the prostitutes spread down from Montmartre and into the 2nd arrondissement; towards the centre of the city along the rue St Denis.

The police, exhibiting Parisian pragmatism, look the other way. Prostitution is sort of illegal in France but, as in most other countries, the authorities turn a fairly blind eye to what goes on just as long as no one frightens the horses.

19th Arrondissement

The most interesting place in the 19th is the bizarrely gothic Parc des Buttes Chaumont. But it's not all that interesting.

20th Arrondissement

The 20th has one 'pièce de résistance' – and what a 'pièce de résistance' it is. The Cimetière du Père Lachaise, which borders on the 11th arrondissement, and which can be reached by taking the Metro to the Père Lachaise stop, is the most extraordinary cemetery in Paris and, quite probably, the entire world. It is absolutely worth a visit. You must go there if you possibly can.

Père Lachaise is famous for its celebrities. It is, for example, where Oscar Wilde and Jim Morrison are buried. (Jim Morrison, by the way, died at no 17 rue Beautreillis, in the 4th arrondissement, though when we last looked there was no sign to commemorate this fact.) It also contains the by now well-rotted corpses of Balzac, Beaumarchais, Chopin, Colette, Delacroix, Eluard, Modigliani, Molière, Edith Piaf and Proust. Ironically, Père Lachaise also contains the body of Sir Sidney Smith who was one of Nelson's admirals.

Of all these the one who brings in most visitors is Morrison. The French get very annoyed that Jim Morrison's grave attracts more visitors than all the rest put together.

It's very easy to get lost in Père Lachaise but we usually manage to find the ex Doors' vocalist's grave by sniff alone. The aroma of marijuana and cheap red wine is unmistakeable. Sadly, the wonderful bust of Jim Morrison has long since disappeared.

The non-celebrity graves are, however, our favourites. (If 'favourite' is the right word.) Some of the inscriptions are heartbreaking. An inconsolable man whose wife died had engraved upon his wife's tomb the words: 'I am waiting to join her. Until I can join her I will simply keep myself occupied. She was loved by everyone whose lives she touched and she will live for ever in the hearts of those who knew her.' Beautiful. True poetry. A tribute worthy of Paris herself.

Appendix 1

Outside Paris

The great Dr Samuel Johnson was once asked by his biographer, the intrepid and faithful Boswell, if he had ever seen the Niagara Falls.

'It is,' said Boswell, 'worth seeing.'

'Worth seeing,' agreed Johnson. 'But not worth going to see.'

The distinction the great man was making is, of course, a valid one. Lots of places and things which are worth seeing and worth visiting are simply not worth going to. The effort of getting there is too great for the reward you receive. An hour spent at Royal Ascot might be fun. But to get there you have to put up with enormous crowds, long queues and the vagaries of a public transport system which passed its best back in the 1950's. It would be nice to visit India or Australia. But the pain of boarding an aircraft and spending 24 hours entombed in a metal cigar where even the air is polluted rather detracts from the pleasure likely to be obtained from actually going there.

There are, of course, heaps of fascinating places outside Paris which are worth seeing. Fontainebleau, Giverny (where Monet lived and painted lilies), Chartres and Chantilly to name but four. But the one place you really should visit (and which is well worth the effort of getting there) is Versailles.

It is reported that 35,000 artisans and skilled craftsmen worked for 40 years to build the Chateau of Versailles. When you see it you will wonder how they did it so quickly.

Go by train. There's a regular train service from Gare St Lazare in Paris and it's quick and cheap. The train station in Versailles is within walking distance of the Chateau. Don't waste time exploring the town, because with occasional exceptions it's a dull, rather battered looking sort of place that gives the impression of being far too much in awe of its main attraction to dare put on its best clothes for visitors.

Appendix 2

Twenty Things
You Must Do In Paris

1. Visit Père Lachaise. Just walk around aimlessly. The Père Lachaise cemetery gives real meaning to the word 'gothic'.

2. Walk around the place des Vosges. Visit on a Sunday when there are most likely to be musicians playing in the cloisters.

3. Admire the Eiffel Tower. Take the lift to the second floor. Afterwards walk in the Champs de Mars and take photographs of the tower. However naff you may think it is you cannot possibly visit Paris without visiting the Eiffel Tower.

4. Have a picnic in the Palais Royale. Buy a baguette, a bottle of wine and other bits and pieces from a local shop.

5. Walk up through Montmartre to Sacre Coeur. Visit the place du Tetre. Yes, it's brash and garish and touristy. But Paris can be. Then walk back down again.

6. Walk along the banks of the Seine and browse among the small bookstalls for old books, old prints and old postcards. Go down to the water's edge and stroll along right by the river.

7. Visit as many famous cafés as you can and have a hot chocolate or a 'vin chaud' in them all. In particular, you must order a 'vin chaud' or a cup of hot chocolate in Les Deux Magots or Café de Flore and watch the world go by for an hour.

8. Go to the Luxembourg Gardens to see the Parisians at play.

9. Go to rue Cler to see typically Parisian small shops.

10. Go to Versailles. Take the train from Gare St Lazare and walk to the Chateau from the station in Versailles.

11. Admire the glass Pyramid at the entrance to the Louvre.

12. Go on a bus tour. Sit on the top of one of the open-topped buses. It sounds touristy and it is. But it's a brilliant way to see

the city. Don't bother going downstairs or in a coach. You won't see half as much. (But if you're sitting on top do watch out for flailing tree branches.)

13. Go into the old Paris Opera building and look at the Marc Chagall ceiling. It's one of the modern wonders of Paris.

14. Visit the Beaubourg in the 4th Arrondisement. It's one of the most remarkable modern buildings in the world and the area around it is certainly lively – if rather touristy.

15. Walk down the Passage Jouffroy and the Passage des Panoramas.

16. Walk from Notre Dame to St Germain des Prés, via the church of St Michel. Visit the Shakespeare and Co bookshop.

17. Go into Galeries Lafayette and admire the atrium.

18. Stroll along the rue de Rivoli.

19. Walk up and down the Champs-Elysées.

20. Visit the Hôtel des Invalides. See Napoleon's tomb and walk around the upper level cloisters surrounding the main court-yard.

Appendix 3

Ten Things Not Worth Doing In Paris

1. Going inside Notre Dame

2. Visiting a flea market. It's a waste of effort. You'll rub shoulders with Japanese, Chinese and American tourists and pickpockets from most of Europe. And see nothing worth buying.

3. Bother queuing to go inside the Louvre unless you're studying art history. It's simply too crowded and the queues are too long.

4. Going inside Sacre Coeur. The outside is much better.

5. Spending a fortune having dinner at Fouquet's, Maxim's or La Tour d'Argent. These aren't anything to do with 'real' Paris. (If you want a treat, buy a cake to accompany your cup of hot chocolate in Les Deux Magots or Café de Flore.)

6. Visit Harry's Bar (in rue Daunou). It's vastly overrated and far more famous than it deserves. Besides, it's the best known meeting place for Americans in Paris. (The last place you want to be.)

7. Don't bother going to see the Opera National de Paris-Bastille. Paris's new opera house, opened in 1989 to celebrate the bicentenary of the storming of the Bastille, is one of the most modern theatres in Europe and is, in our view, something of a joke.

8. Don't bother visiting the Arc de Triomphe de l'Etoile. It's best viewed from the bottom of the Champs-Elysées. And you'll get a wonderful aerial view of Paris when you go up the Eiffel Tower.

9. Don't bother visiting the Bois de Boulogne. It has become rather seedy and, to be honest, not particularly safe. It simply isn't worth the effort it takes to get there.

10. Don't bother taking a trip in a boat on the river. You can see Paris much more freely by walking along the banks. Just make sure you have a map with you so that you can identify the various buildings along the edges of the Seine. (And, remember, the best way to get an overview of Paris is to take a ride on the top deck of one of the sightseeing buses.)

Also by Vernon Coleman

Paris in My Springtime

"A little while ago, while sorting through some boxes I found in the attic, I came across a diary I had kept during a stay in Paris in the last part of 1963 and the first months of 1964. In September of 1963 I had started medical school. But I'd been taken ill and had to temporarily abandon my studies. With the best part of a year to kill I was given two choices: I could either stay at home and get a temporary job driving a fish delivery van or I could go to Paris. After a great deal of thought (which, on reflection, must have taken very nearly a second) I chose to go to Paris. And this is the story of what happened to me that year. Or is it?"

Vernon Coleman

"Your books – both fiction and non fiction – are an absolute tonic." Mr R.W., Sussex

"Just want to thank you for all your wonderful books. Will be buying more soon." M.A., Surrey

"Having read three of your marvellous books so far – I have several more recently purchased to read with great anticipation. I felt I had to tell you how much I enjoyed them." Miss S.H., Exeter

Hardback £12.99
Published by Chilton Designs
Order from Publishing House • Trinity Place • Barnstaple •
Devon EX32 9HG • England
Telephone 01271 328892 • Fax 01271 328768
www.vernoncoleman.com

Also by Vernon Coleman

It's Never Too Late

Tony Davison is bored, tired and fed up with life. He has lost his job and his wife, and doesn't have much of a future. In despair, he sells his house and most of his belongings and sets off to Paris for a weekend holiday. But what started off as a quick holiday break soon turns into a once-in-a-lifetime experience.

It's Never Too Late tells the uplifting story of Tony's search for a new life and happiness in a new country. Full of the gentle humour and anecdotes which are so much the hallmark of Vernon Coleman's novels.

"Imagine that you feel like settling down in a comfortable armchair with an entertaining book – one that will keep your attention and combat the desire to nod off ... If this description fits you then you could do much worse than spoil yourself with this book. The author's style is both easy to read and makes you want to keep turning the pages – in fact I had to force myself to stop reading and put the book down. I am sure you will enjoy the book, which apart from anything else brings to life the atmosphere of Paris – so why not give it to a loved one or friend ... and promptly borrow it to read yourself!? Whatever you may decide, we have chosen this as our Book of the Month."
LIVING FRANCE

"*It's Never Too Late* is a light-hearted reversal of the ageing process." FRANCE MAGAZINE

Hardback £12.99
Published by Chilton Designs
Order from Publishing House • Trinity Place • Barnstaple •
Devon EX32 9HG • England
Telephone 01271 328892 • Fax 01271 328768
www.vernoncoleman.com

For a catalogue of Vernon Coleman's books
please write to:

Publishing House
Trinity Place
Barnstaple
Devon EX32 9HG
England

Telephone	01271 328892
Fax	01271 328768

Outside the UK:

Telephone	+44 1271 328892
Fax	+44 1271 328768

Or visit our website:

www.vernoncoleman.com